SOUTHERN · TIMES ·

Contents

The Transport Treasury

TIMES SERIES

On 3 September 1983, the Somerset & Dorset Railway Trust recreated the 'Pines Express' at the Bluebell Railway – appropriately using 75027, an ex-S&D loco. The late Donald Beale and Peter Smith, both well-known as S&D enginemen, have come for the day and are seen here with guard Nick Stanbury.
Brian Macdermott

Front Cover: Bo-Bo electric, later Class 71 No E5004 at Shortlands Junction with a Victoria – Dover service. The location is where the Catloop Loop line joins the Chatham main line. *Ken Wightman / Transport Treasury*

Rear cover: No 30911 *Dover* but at Farnborough with what is likely a stopping train for Salisbury. Track circuiting has meant that occupancy of the section ahead of the signal has automatically returned the starting signals to 'On'.

Copies of images used within SOUTHERN TIMES and sourced from the Transport Treasury archive are available for purchase/download. Please quote the Issue, article, page number, and if shown the reference.

In addition the Transport Treasury Archive contains tens of thousands of other UK, Irish and some European railway photographs.

© Images and design: The Transport Treasury 2022.

ISBN 978-1-913251-34-5

First Published in 2022 by Transport Treasury Publishing Ltd.,
16 Highworth Close, High Wycombe, HP13 7PJ

www.ttpublishing.co.uk *or for editorial issues and contributions email to* **SouthernTimes@email.com**

Printed in the Malta by the Gutenberg Press.

Important Notice; due to circumstances outside our control we regret the cover price of SOUTHERN TIMES will increase from 1 January 2023.

INTRODUCTION

For the first words of this issue we have started on a theme which we hope others care to continue; that of the 'Guest Editorial'. As we have mentioned in issue 2, we ('we' – meaning the team at Transport Treasury) have been humbled by the response to this new series and consequently we welcome the opportunity for others to become involved.

If you would like to similarly put pen to paper (or even quill to parchment), do please get in touch, we look forward to hearing from you.

Robin Fell and the team at Transport Treasury

Guest Editorial 'My Southern Times'
by Nick Stanbury

My family had no railway background, although my grandfather had more than a passing interest, especially in the Great Western, whose broad-gauge conversion in the Plymouth area he had witnessed in 1892 at the age of eight. My introduction to railways was more prosaic – a line and a station at the bottom of the garden; Fulwell on the ex-LSWR Shepperton branch. As one of the first routes electrified in 1916, its passenger services were unexciting but the daily goods train – invariably hauled by a Drummond 700 (often with a crew bicycle carried on the tender top) – provided a welcome steam interlude.

There was no car in the family, so our outings were always made by public transport. The station was of course very convenient, as were the two trolleybus routes served by the nearby Fulwell Depot – amongst the last to go in London in 1962. I became used to travelling into and around London, and sometimes

Above and overleaf: Fulwell Station c1952, with the morning Shepperton goods from Feltham via Twickenham. The Drummond 700 is apparently 30696 (a Feltham stalwart), probably on Duty 133. Nick Stanbury looks on with his grandfather and was suitably inspired by the guard's cheery wave to serve as a guard on the Bluebell Railway for 53 years from 1965. *Photos by the late H. N. Stanbury, © N. H. & P. J. Stanbury*

further afield when we went on holiday or for outings. Seaside trips via Raynes Park to Bognor or Littlehampton in a galloping unit were a regular summer jaunt. By the time I started at grammar school in 1960, I was a seasoned traveller, so my daily 'commute' from Fulwell via Richmond to Ravenscourt Park held no terrors. Although the District Line provided the service beyond Richmond, the route still showed many signs of its LSWR origins. This and many other aspects of the railways in and around West London cemented my growing interest in railway history and operation – particularly that relating to the Southern and its connections and joint interests, especially the Somerset & Dorset. In 1965, I was a founder member of the erstwhile Somerset & Dorset Circle (now the Somerset & Dorset Railway Trust).

I had also developed a keen interest in model railways and did my best to produce a layout located in S&D territory, as my limited funds and skills allowed. Real progress on that front had to wait for a number of years and a more spacious home and deeper pocket. Meanwhile, following a Whitsun 1965 visit to

the Bluebell Railway, I realised that I could – and should – get involved in hands-on railway work and promptly joined the voluntary staff.

I was soon passed out as a passenger guard, a position I held continuously until 'retirement' in 2018, and also worked as a goods guard and shunter, and for several years as the Bluebell's first Guards' Inspector. I also served on the Society's management committee in the early 1970s and was subsequently closely involved in the Northern Extension project.

I qualified as a chartered accountant in 1972 and moved to Brighton to run a new office for my partnership. My house there also had a railway – albeit the recently closed Kemp Town branch – at the bottom of the garden. In 1978 a move across the town had me overlooking the main line opposite Lovers Walk. Hence I went from LSWR to LBSCR, but since 2000 have lived in West Kent in SER territory, with the Hastings line just out of sight. In retirement, I maintain my interest in most things Southern and in British railway history and operation generally. My two sons do not actively share my interests, alas, but the signs with my grandchildren are encouraging!

Droxford Pre-WW1

We are delighted to feature one of Sean Bolan's superlative views of the Edwardian railway scene with this painting of a Down Stokes Bay train entering Droxford in Edwardian days. Sean is renowned for the painstaking research and accuracy he puts into his work and this shows his skills to advantage; notwithstanding the amount of time of necessity spent on repetitive detail – the fencing for example. So far as the actual location is concerned, Droxford was one of five intermediate stations on the Meon Valley line between Alton and Fareham; a 22 mile route opened as late as 1903 and laid out to main line standards. As to why it was actually built, through sparsely populated rural Hampshire, remains an enigma; a blocking line, a faster and quicker route to Stokes Bay for the ferry to the Isle of Wight, perhaps both of these and other reasons as well. Suffice to say the railway never came close to being any sort of financial success with economies taking place even before grouping. Probably Droxford's greatest claim to fame was when Winston Churchill and the other Allied leaders of WW2 came to the station to discuss plans for invasion prior to D-Day. In later years, and certainly not on a par with the previous event, part of the then truncated route was used for the making of an advert for a particular brand of confectionery; readers of a certain age may recall, 'All because the lady loves…..'. (Our hero seen jumping off an overbridge on to the roof of a moving train.) After all services ceased, Droxford was for a short time the hub of an abortive preservation attempt and also the home base of the private enterprise Sadler Vectrail project, a hoped for means of reviving rail fortunes on the Isle of Wight and possibly elsewhere by using a bus/ coach type vehicle operating on rails.

None of these would secure the future of Droxford as both through goods and passenger services had ceased in February 1955 although some goods continued to be dealt with at the now truncated Droxford terminus into the 1960s.

Not surprisingly the site fell into disuse after the preservationists and entrepreneur left but was fortunately rescued and restored as a delightful country retreat. Conscious of its place in history, one time owner Tony Williams went so far as to build a new signal box in identical fashion to its former design but this time made into a guest bedroom suite. There may not be any trains to Stokes Bay a century on from Sean's painting, but without doubt the memory lives on.

Top: We start not with a scrap view – although it so nearly might have been – but instead with the remains of No 852 *Sir Walter Raleigh* outside Eastleigh works after the rear portion of the frames had been cut through and the boiler removed. This was the engine that received the direct hit through the cab from an enemy bomb at Nine Elms. Such damage would ordinarily have seen the engine scrapped but the unreliable behaviour of the new 'Merchant Navy' class engines meant repairs were authorised. The class therefore entered British Railways in 1948 service intact.

Bottom: No 30856 *Lord St Vincent* fresh from overhaul at Eastleigh in September 1960 – destined also to be its final works visit. This engine would survive a further two years.

The demise of the 'Lord Nelson' class

The death knell for the Lord Nelson class was rung some miles away from their then current haunts on the Western Section of the Southern Region and may be easily identified with Phase 1 and subsequently Phase 2 of the Kent Coast Electrification; respectively in 1959 and 1962.

Electrification and/or dieselisation of passenger and freight services on the Eastern Section meant steam would no longer have a part to play and in consequence there were both mass withdrawals and similarly mass transfers of now redundant steam stock to the only area where steam remained dominant; the lines out of Waterloo.

Here is not the place to debate what were in some cases little more than 'paper transfers'. 'Motive Power' on the Western section certainly willing to take over modern locomotives but they had little use for the multitude of former SECR and Southern 4-4-0 and 0-6-0 tender engines similarly now with no work available to them. The SE section had also operated a number of Bulleid and Standard 5 types and these were willingly accepted and similarly cascaded on to the Western Section lines.

Stephen Townroe in his 1973 work 'The Arthurs, Nelsons & Schools at Work' (Ian Allan) aptly describes what follows, '…to the accompaniment of pressure from the British Railways Board to reduce the steam locomotive fleet, the 'Arthurs', 'Nelsons' and 'Schools' were withdrawn from normal service at the end of 1962'. (Elsewhere Townroe makes the point it might even have been considered surprising the Lord Nelson class survived at all the post war commensurate with the building of so many Pacifics.)

For now we are concerned here only with the Lord Nelson class where inroads into their numbers had started in May 1961 when No 30863 was withdrawn.

Prior to this all 16 of the class had been based at Eastleigh, some since 1949 although the final three, including No 30863, did not arrive until 1959. Having all the members of one class based at the one depot was slightly unusual but had been at the instigation of Stephen Townroe who then occupied the position of District Motive Power Superintendent and who we know was without doubt a Maunsell fan. (Pre-war, 11 had also been based at Battersea for Eastern Section workings.)

Townroe was certainly not anti-Bulleid but he was a practical man only too aware that on a good day a Bulleid Pacific in its original form was without equal, but the next day on the same duty, with the same type of coal and with the same crew it could be a totally different proposition. With Eastleigh responsible for the running of the Up Boat trains from Southampton in what were deemed 'Q' paths (paths within the working timetable where an additional service might be slotted), it was essential to have at his disposal an engine that was predictable and thus able to operate such services without causing undue delay to other workings.

Townroe thus secured the allocation of most and eventually all the class to Eastleigh and where the men could also now become familiar with the class and the firing method needed to cope with a long but narrow firebox. There was an added issue for the fireman in that the grate of the Lord Nelson was flat for part of its length and then sloped down and forward. Consequently it was all too easy for too much – or too little coal – to end up either at the front or on the level section. In either case steaming would be quickly affected and the only recourse was judicious use of the fire irons, hardly easy on a moving train. Elsewhere 4-6-0s running both on the Southern and on other railways/regions never seemed to be regularly plagued with such steaming difficulties whilst one example of a class having a grate similar to that of the Lord

Left: Whilst at Eastleigh the class saw regular use on boat trains both to and from Southampton. Headboards were also carried on a number of services including this slightly unusual version of 'The Cunarder'. *Les Elsey*

Bottom: The more normal rectangular board is seen attached to No 30859 *Lord Hood* waiting at Canute Road on 1 April 1957 to reverse back to Eastleigh having brought in a down special. The train had left Waterloo at 9.35am, one of two boat trains running that day, one in each direction. No 30859 had been in charge of 11 vehicles including three Pullman cars on the way south with passengers embarking at Southampton on to *RMS Alcantara*. The engine allocated for the down journey would usually have worked up to Waterloo or Nine Elms with an ordinary working, a similar procedure applying for up trains. This way excessive light engine mileage was avoided. *Tony Molyneaux*

Opposite: In the opposite direction a few weeks later, No 30853 *Sir Richard Grenville* has a full head of steam ready for the its main line run from Southampton to Waterloo on Sunday 23 June 1957, Copious amounts of baggage was the norm for passengers travelling by liner and which explains the three utility vans. According to the Special Traffic Notice for the week, this was a 10.45am departure from Southampton with passengers off the *RMS Andes*. It was listed as running with 14 vehicles including four Pullman cars which may explain why the fireman was keen to have a good head of steam from the start for the weight of the train behind the tender. *Tony Molyneaux*

Nelson type was the former LNWR 'Claughton' class but - there were 130 of these so familiarity was not an issue.

Indeed this lack of familiarity with the LN class was likely a far more accurate way to describe why the type as a whole has received a bad press over the years; simply put there were not enough of them. With only a few engines, plans for a further 16 prior to WW2 had been cancelled and were never resurrected, it was said due to financial constraints. (Perhaps available funds were indeed being concentrated into electrification so giving rise

to the tales that steam had indeed been the poor relation in the 1930s.)

Too few engines spread too thinly added to an already poor reputation, the efforts of a King Arthur often exceeding what might be achieved with their larger cousin. Being perfectly honest the class were certainly not perfect and performed far better after the various modifications made under Mr Bulleid. Even so far from now reaching a peak and deserved positive reputation, they now existed even in their improved state under the shadow of Mr Bulleid's own designs; this might indeed be a fitting epitaph 'living in the shadow of others'.

With more seemingly present on the debit side let us try and even the score somewhat for certainly as regards their build they were to a design that required little attention to the main frames compared with others. Indeed the main frames remained in better condition throughout their lives than other Southern 4-6-0 types and also the later BR Standard designs, certainly far better than the King class on the neighbouring GWR. As if to prove the point four of the class, Nos 30851/9/62/3 went for scrap without ever having received any attention to main frames during the whole of their lives. At first sight this might appear to be explained as the LN class were four-cylinder

engines and so perhaps less stress was created compared with an engine having just two outside cylinders, but this cannot be the whole explanation for the 'King' type were also four-cylinder machines. Instead we should instead look at design and build and praise both rather than condemn all without justification.

In addition to their boat train work from Southampton, whilst based at Eastleigh the class were also regular performers on the top-link Eastleigh turns as well as Inter-Regional workings from Bournemouth via Basingstoke and Reading to Oxford. At the latter point the engine would be turned and serviced ready for the return working.

Other duties included van trains between Waterloo or Nine Elms and Southampton, the latter duties included as part of the normal diagram. An Eastleigh based member of the class would also stand-by at Southampton Central until the down 'Bournemouth Belle' had satisfactorily departed just in case the engine in charge of the prestige service were ailing. Assuming there no issues the Lord Nelson would attach itself to a short stopping train which it then worked through to Bournemouth. Chris Richardson, a former Eastleigh fireman in the early 1960s recalls a Lord Nelson being used on a fitted permanent way train from

Redbridge to Basingstoke, the turn made unpleasant by the driver he was with.

This then was the situation up to 1961 when with more and more Bulleid Pacifics available and with more predictable performance available with the rebuilt Bulleid engines, so the Lord Nelson class appear to have been side-lined. There were some crews who would prefer a Lord Nelson although with various class members coming up to a due date for heavy repairs it was likely not all were in pristine mechanical condition.

In Southern Railway days heavy repairs appear to have been undertaken at two to two and a half yearly intervals although this timescale was expanded during the 1950s to every five years – perhaps on the basis of mileage rather than time. An example is 36 months for No 30852 and no less than double that for No 30859 at 72 months; mileage worked would appear to be the only explanation. Speaking of mileage, final figures are not available for the whole class but on average they seem to have covered around 1.3 million miles each which equated to an annual mileage in the order 35,000 miles each. Less than a Great Western 'King' which was of similar age but then the latter's services were invariably over longer distances. We should also recall the words of at least one correspondent to the 'Railway Observer' who noted that when visiting Eastleigh in the 1950s there always seemed to be several examples of the class 'sat around'.

Bear in mind too with Eastleigh responsibility for providing locomotive power for many of the boat trains both from and sometimes to Southampton Docks, it was necessary to hold motive power in reserve for when these train ran. A situation that would continue almost to the end of the class's existence. Indeed, and again quoting from the 'R.O'. this time from April 1962, when a correspondent noted a member of the class could still be seen at the head of a boat train but nowadays (1962) usually when no Pacific was available.

Even at this late stage there was also other work available including the 6.04am Southampton terminus to Waterloo and 7.22am Eastleigh to Waterloo although in both cases a Nelson would only appear if for whatever reason a Pacific was not available. Perhaps this sporadic usage of the survivors, allied once again to unfamiliarity and perhaps even general condition may have contributed to a 70 minute delay attributable to No 30857 when in charge with the 5.09pm Waterloo to Basingstoke passenger service – a train which would normally arrive at Basingstoke at 6.27pm. 'Shortage of steam' appeared on the official report. It was also somewhat ironic, that same report on No 30857 again from the 'R.O.' had as its next heading a reference to a new form of traction, the Electro-Diesels.

The following month the 'R.O.' referred to the dwindling fleet of Maunsell 4-6-0 passenger types but added that Nos 30862 and 30861 had been observed on the down 'Cunarder' and a Bournemouth passenger service respectively.

It would probably also be fair to say the Lord Nelson class appeared to work solidly but away from the limelight. Consequently only a very few enthusiast tours are noted involving the class in their final two years, one in 1961 and two in 1962 (to be strictly accurate one of the latter was repeated by the same society and to the same destination – Swindon – so we may count it as just one). The 1962 events are all the surprising as it cannot fail to have been noticed that at the start of the year almost half the class had already fallen by the wayside.

The 1961 trip saw No 30861 at the head of the first part of the Locomotive Club of Great Britain 'Solent Limited' from Waterloo to Portsmouth; the remainder of the tour taking place around south Hampshire, thence to Newbury and finally back to Waterloo hauled by a variety of different engines.

In 1962 it was turn of No 30850 to work the Home Counties Railway Society special from Paddington to Swindon and return twice; on 3 June and again three weeks later on 24 June. Finally on 2 September No 30861 was used for the Southern Counties Touring Society 'South Western Limited' from Waterloo to Sidmouth

No 30850 *Lord Nelson* on another boat special from Southampton, again including a number of Pullman cars, recorded in Shawford cutting on 16 May 1958. Due to the prevailing weather conditions, tides and in consequence unpredictable berthing times, boat train specials were difficult to schedule, this particular service must have been a short notice special as no details of its working appears in the weekly Special Traffic Notices. *Tony Molyneaux*

Junction and then return from Exeter as far back as Salisbury. No 30861 along with No 30862 as the last pair still (on paper at least) active were withdrawn one month later.

Official records giving withdrawal dates also show two other interesting points. The first that some engines appear to have been stored for a time prior to withdrawal and secondly that the period between withdrawal and cutting-up was in most cases very short often a matter of weeks. Of the 15 engines disposed of (No 30850 was saved for the National collection), two were also reduced to scrap at Ashford. With all the engines withdrawn from Eastleigh it begs the question how did they get there, although we know one at least did work a (non-passenger) train almost to its graveyard. Presumably the reason being Ashford had spare (scrapping) capacity at the time.

The Lord Nelson class appears to have faded from the limelight quietly and without much ceremony. Apart from No 30850 only one class member made it into 1963 and that was at Ashford where No 30852 was stored pending scrap for over 12 months, consequently with preservation still very much its infancy there was nothing left to consider saving later.

The year 1962 was a bad one for steam not just as per the comment by Stephen Townroe earlier but as it also witnessed the demise of so many other Southern types including the 'K' class moguls, various Brighton tanks and the 3-cylinder Maunsell moguls. As if to expand this depressing perspective, the successors to the Lord Nelson class on their various working, namely the Bulleid Light Pacifics would also start to see inroads into their own numbers the very next year 1963.

With hindsight it was probably best to go when all was calm and not suffer the indignity of lack of maintenance and external filth that typified steam in the last years and last months.

Acknowledgements: Gerry Nichols (SLS), Chris Richardson.

Bibliography:

Locomotives of the Southern Railway Part 1. D L Bradley. RCTS 1975

Maunsell's Nelsons. D W Winkworth. George Allen & Unwin.1980

The Book of the Lord Nelson 4-6-0s. Richard Derry. Irwell Press 2005.

The Railway Observer RCTS, various issues

The Railway Magazine, various issues.

	Last Repair	Date withdrawn	Final Allocation	Mileage	Disposal details	Last General repair
30850	Light intermediate 1-12 to 31-12-60	18-8-62	Eastleigh since 1949	1,349,617		1957
30851	Light Casual 18-10 to 26-10-61	23-12-61	Eastleigh Since 1949	1,296,146	Stored Elh Wks 10-61 to 4-62 Cut up Elh w/e 5-5-62	1955
30852	Light Intermediate 12-8 to 3-9-60	17-2-62	Eastleigh Since 1949	1,249,831	Stored Ashford 2-62 cut up Ashford w/e 10-3-62	1958
30853	Light Intermediate 1-4 to 30-4-60	3-3-62	Eastleigh Since 1949		Stored Elh Works 2-3-62 cut up w/e 21-4-62	1954/5
30854	Light Casual 14-6 to 25-6-60	9-9-61	Eastleigh Since 1949		Cut up Elh w/e 30-9-61	1957
30855	Heavy Intermediate 25-5 to 18-6-60	9-9-61	Eastleigh Since 1950	1,239,589	Stored Elh Works 9-61 to 1-62 cut up w/e 10-2-62	1958
30856	General 5-8 to 10-9-60	22-9-62	Eastleigh Since 1950		Stored Elh Works 9-10-62 cut up w/e 17-11-62	As last repair
30857	Non Classified 22-5 to 26-5-62	22-9-62	Eastleigh Since 1950		Stored Elh Works 9-62 cut up w/e 20-10-62	1960
30858	Light Casual 19-8 to 3-9-62	19-8-61	Eastleigh Since 1958		Stored Elh Works 8-10-61 cut up w/e 25-11-61	1956
30859	Light Casual 5-3 to 25-3-61	9-12-61	Eastleigh Since 1958		Stored Elh Works 10-11=61 Cut up Elh w/e 23-12-61	1959
30860	Non Classified 22/23-12-61	11-8-62	Eastleigh Since 1959	1,347,841	Stored Elh Works 8-62 Cut up Elh w/e 1-9-62	1960
30861	Light Casual 3-1 to 27-1-62	6-10-62	Eastleigh Since 1956		Stored Elh Works 9-10-62 Cut up Elh w/e 24-11-62	1959
30862	Heavy Intermediate 21-4 to 13-5-61	6-10-62	Eastleigh Since 1956	1,390,329	Cut up Elh w/e 27-10-62	1958
30863	Heavy Casual 1-2 to 10-3-61	10-2-62	Eastleigh Since 1956		Stored at Ashford 2-62 cut up Ashford w/e 24-2-62	1957
30864	Light Intermediate 1-10 to 31-10-59	27-1-62	Eastleigh Since 1959		Stored Elh Works 1-2-62 Cut up Elh w/e 10-3-62	1956
30865	10-2 to 28-2-1959	30-5-61	Eastleigh Since 1959		Stored Elh Works 5-7-61 Cut up Elh w/e 2-9-61	1955/6

Passenger working for either No 30852 or 30862, at Bournemouth West. The headcode is for a Waterloo service whilst alongside is an inter-regional train, the latter type of working the class would also regularly perform between Bournemouth and Oxford.

Bournemouth depot plays host to two members of the class, Nos 30863 and 30850. The enlarged Bulleid chimney may be noted.

As one correspondence to the 'Railway Observer' noted, there would always seem to be some members of the class waiting around Eastleigh, exemplified here by No 30851 but devoid of its *Sir Francis Drake* nameplate. Ordinarily this might signify the engine had been withdrawn but we cannot be certain as the photograph was taken on 2 July 1961 and the engine was not withdrawn until December. *Tony Molyneaux*

Still with No 30851 but this time perhaps not so hopeful as it stands within a line of other engines. Stored perhaps and unlikely to steam again. *The Transport Treasury*

Not perhaps typical 'Nelson' duty, but an example of the sort of working the class could find themselves on to balance a boat train turn. No 30856 *Lord St. Vincent* at Clapham Junction on 10 May 1962 with the 7.35pm Nine Elms to Southampton goods. *Leslie Freeman / The Transport Treasury*

Special duty for No 30856 *Lord St Vincent* south of Petersfield with the LCGB 'Solent Limited' of 30 April 1961. Just six coaches suggests that even at this time in their lives the class were playing second-fiddle to other types. *Tony Molyneaux*

Opposite top: Arrived at Portsmouth Harbour and with the other type of 'Nelson' alongside. *A E Bennett / The Transport Treasury*

Opposite bottom: The final special run by a member of the class was on 2 September 1962 when No 30861 *Lord Anson* powered an SCTS train from Waterloo to Sidmouth Junction and then the return from Exeter Central as far as Salisbury. The engine is seen here leaving Exeter Central, also the final time a member of the class would be seen here in BR days. *S C Nash / Stephenson Locomotive Society*

This page, top: Cold and lifeless at Eastleigh on 9 September 1961. No 30858 had been withdrawn three weeks earlier and from similar images appear to have remained in the same spot for several weeks. The chalked board at the front refers to 'Bosh… …on'. *Tony Molyneaux*

This page: bottom: Heading to its own demise. No 30863 *Lord Rodney* with an engineer's train passing Knockholt on 3 February 1962 en-route to Ashford where it would later be cut-up. Although not officially withdrawn (on paper at least) until 10 February, it is highly unlikely it returned to its Eastleigh home. Southern Region management were determined to utilise the engine to its maximum on what was also its final journey. *S C Nash / |Stephenson Locomotive Society*

Opposite top: A trio of members of the class, Nos 30856, 30861 and one other at the front of Eastleigh works on their way to the rear where they will be disposed of. Two tenders from Lord Nelson class engines were salvaged and attached to Schools class engines until they too were withdrawn; that from No 30854 went to No 30921, and from No 30865 to No 30912. Rods were not removed for the final short journey from the running shed. *John Click*

Opposite bottom: Around the back of Eastleigh works, No 30857 awaits the attention of the cutters. *Roger Thornton*

This page, top: A similar fate will befall No 30862 but not before one of its *Lord Collingwood* nameplates had been removed by a ground of cleaners / fireman from the running shed for subsequent formal presentation to Stephen (Collingwood) Townroe. *Roger Thornton*

This page, bottom: And so we end in similar vein to whence we started, except this time there was no reprise. What had once been No 30860 *Lord Hawke* in the course of being dismembered at the rear of Eastleigh works on 10 September 1962. *Roger Thornton*

Abnormal load movement
Sunday 22 January 1956

So how do you move an out of gauge load around the Southern Region? Without stating the obvious – very carefully. In fact with a considerable degree of planning and in the case of this particular load, overnight on Sunday 22 January 1956.

The load in question was a 124 ton transformer, not excessively heavy by train load standards but awkward and similarly indivisible.

It had commenced its journey from sidings at Hollinwood, Manchester and was destined for the British Electricity Authority (sic) siding at Marchwood on the Fawley branch on the west side of Southampton water.

Once the details had been worked out, as was customary for the period a Special Traffic Notice was issued covering the movement from the WR at Reading West Junction and where the Southern Region would assume responsibility though to Basingstoke and

thence via Eastleigh to the destination. Despite the distance being little more than 50 miles, the schedule was such that in excess of 10 hours was shown for the journey commencing at 12.20am. (We are not given details of the journey from Manchester to Reading.)

This time is explained as the maximum speed at any point should not exceed 15mph whilst at certain locations – detailed later – this was reduced to just 3mph.

The 'abnormal' aspect of the load was the width, a maximum of 13' 4". To accommodate this the actual load was placed so that the overhand was on the 'six-foot' side between Reading and as far as Totton. From Totton, the final distance to Marchwood, it was on the cess side.

Including the locomotive involved, which we know was a 350hp diesel shunter, the consist was:

Diesel locomotive
Brake van (vacuum fitted)
SR tool van DS252
Brake van
Transformer trolley No 901800
Tool van
Brake van.

The vacuum pipes were connected between the locomotive and the first two vehicles as far as Southampton Junction.

Some of the instructions given might today seem obvious, but even if this were a clearly well rehearsed procedure they were still included. 'No traffic of any description must be allowed to pass or be passed by the load on an adjacent track on either side throughout the journey. Trains may be allowed to pass where an unoccupied track exists between the train and the load, such trains must not convey out of gauge loads.'

Emergency berthing arrangements were also notified with 'No 2 Down siding' at Winchester and at Eastleigh 'short road via Eastleigh Yard ground frame'. Named (mostly) Traffic Inspectors were also on duty; with the train it was Inspector Norman, at Basingstoke it was the 'London West District Inspector', at Winchester Inspector Capon, whilst at Southampton Junction was Inspector Southwell and Assistant Chief P/Way Inspector Burnett, the latter would also supervise the train through to Marchwood.

Several signal boxes normally closed/switched out in the early hours of Sunday morning were also to be opened: Mortimer, Medstead, Alresford, Winchester Junction, Shawford Junction, Swaythling, Millbrook, Lyndhurst Road, and Marchwood. Some of these might appear strange as they were not on the route involved but are explained as per diversions and altered timings of other services.

Two signal alterations were also required, the first the temporary removal of a ground signal located in the 'six foot' at the station end of Blechynden tunnel, and the second where the front 'blinder' to the green glass of the lower arm of Totton Up starting signal was to be removed.

Most interesting of all was the apparent ability to move the load by a small amount to one side or the other. The distances involved quote movements of up to 12 inches but as to how this was achieved is not mentioned. Examples of where it was required were Litchfield Tunnel and Popham Tunnel '…move load before passing. Train to proceed with caution…7 mph. …'. The timetable shows a minimum of 20 minutes was required for this operation and which took place when the train was stationary.

In addition to the special, two regular late evening services were affected by revised timings on the day prior to the move, and 14 overnight and in the early morning of Sunday 22nd. Two 'Q' paths between Southampton Docks and Waterloo were also deemed as 'Pathway not available.'

Look out for Southern Times Issue 4 in early 2023.

Content to include:

The Drummond 'Paddleboxes'

Southern allocations: Reading, Redhill, St Leonards and Tonbridge

Track spreading by Leader - proven?

A privileged visitor; the footplate rides of John Davenport

Southern termini in colour

West of Exeter

Stephen Townroe's colour archive

Notes on driving

A Surrey-Sussex Line: Horsham to Guildford Part 2

and of course lots more!

The Deptford Branch, Part 2
Alan Postlethwaite

In Issue 2 of *Southern Times* we looked at both ends of the branch. This second part unravels the Cold Blow Tangle of branch lines to the north of New Cross Gate. We are indebted to John J. Smith for taking the trouble to photograph the area so thoroughly, also to both John and the Bluebell Railway archivists (all voluntary workers) for making this and other collections available to us. John Smith was a BR employee with access to most parts of the railway and with knowledge of freight, empty stock and special workings. The only problem being to sometimes interpret the abbreviations in his notes!

Top: There were two Up lines at the start of the branch. Cold Blow Lane crossed the lower line on the level and then passed under the upper line. Cold Blow farmhouse was on the left just beyond the far bridge which carries the Brighton main line. *John J. Smith, Bluebell Railway Archives, 1965*

Bottom: Demolition of Cold Blow signal works. It doesn't look big enough to handle posts or brackets but it does appear to have a forge. It is likely that castings and wooden/ pressed steel arms were brought here for painting and sub-assembly. *John J. Smith, Bluebell Railway Archives, 1965*

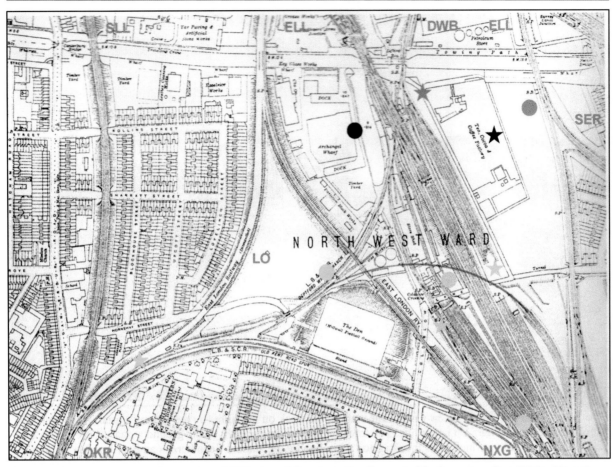

Superimposed on the Ordnance Survey Map of 1913, the **red line** shows the alignment of the former spur from Old Kent Road to the Down side of New Cross Gate. It crossed the Deptford Wharf lower Up line on the level, clearly a nuisance and probably the reason for dismantling it.

Red and Yellow Stars: The Deptford Wharf Down line was reversible. Cold Blow farmhouse was to the right of the yellow star.

Blue Dot: The Deptford Wharf upper Up line was also reversible. It carried most of the Deptford Wharf traffic from New Cross Gate.

Blue Star: The Deptford Wharf lower Up line was also reversible. It ran from the sunken coal yard at New Cross Gate.

Black Dot: The stub of the Croydon Canal serving Archangel Wharf and a timber yard.

Black Star: The Mazawattee tea factory opened in 1900 and closed in 1953. Its clock tower was a landmark across the marshes.

DWB: The Deptford Wharf Branch.

ELL: The East London Line to and from Deptford Road Junction.

LO: This spur from Old Kent Road to Deptford Road Junction was rebuilt ca 2010 as the London Overground line to Highbury & Islington.

OKR: Old Kent Road Junction. The nearby station closed in 1917.

NXG: The top end of New Cross Gate station.

SER: The East London line from Canal Bridge Junction (**red dot**) to New Cross (SER) station.

SLL: The South London Line to South Bermondsey.

New Cross Stadium occupied the LO triangle from 1933 until 1969, offering greyhound racing, speedway and stock car racing at different times. The stadium was also used during the war for fund-raising fairs to build warships.

Millwall played football at The Den from 1910 until 1993 when they moved to a new ground near South Bermondsey station.

Opposite top: This is taken from the blue star on the OS map. The Deptford Wharf lower Up line crossed Cold Blow Lane on the level, then passed the signal works before curving right to pass under the Brighton main line. Top right is a glimpse of the Mazawattee clock tower. *John J. Smith, Bluebell Railway, 1965*

Opposite bottom: This is taken from the green dot on the map, showing demolition of the Old Kent Road - Deptford Wharf spur where it passed under the East London Up line. The right-hand span of the bridge once led to a small gas works that produced kitchen car gas from oil. The signal works is on the far right and the Mazawattee clock tower stands tall in the distance. But who lived in the house? *John J. Smith, Bluebell Railway Archives, 1965*

This page, top: This is taken from the blue dot on the OS map where the Deptford Wharf upper Up spur starts its descent to cross under the Brighton main line. The foreground bridge is where the Old Kent Road spur once passed beneath to the Down side of New Cross Gate. The crane is on the stub of the Croydon Canal and the dilapidated shed may once have belonged to Cold Blow Farm. Standard class 4MT 2-6-4 tank No. 80019 is heading empty Bulleid stock. John's notes show the train as working from London Bridge to New Cross Gate. Its route (avoiding a clash with Brighton main line traffic) was via NXG (Down side) - Deptford Wharf - NXG (Up side), reversing twice. *John J. Smith, Bluebell Railway Archives, 1965*

This page, bottom: This is taken from the green star on the OS map. Stopped at the Home signals of Old Kent Road Junction, class E4 tank No 32471 hauls what John describes as the 11.06 New Cross Gate - DKN. To interpret this, the 'D' is likely to stand for Deptford Wharf since that is the direction from which the train is coming. The 'KN' is most probably Kensington with reversal at Victoria or Battersea. *John J. Smith, Bluebell Railway Archives, 1954*

This page, top: This is taken from the yellow dot on the OS map where the East London Up line (*right*) passes Millwall football stadium. LMS 2-6-4 tank class 4P No 42087 is bringing empty birdcage stock off the (reversible) Old Kent Road spur, en route from Eardley sidings to New Cross Gate via Tulse Hill and Peckham Rye. The Eardley carriage complex is noticeably absent from railway publications. *John J. Smith, Bluebell Railway Archives, 1954*

This page, bottom: This is taken from the yellow star on the OS map with the lift bridge in the distance. Class E6 tank No 32415 is hauling a long coal train from Deptford Wharf up the incline towards New Cross Gate. The sidings are holding overflow stock from Deptford Wharf. The Mazawattee tea factory on the right did not use the railway but they did use zebras for a while on delivery vans. *John J. Smith, Bluebell Railway Archives, 1957*

Opposite top: The original lift bridge over the Grand Surrey Canal was hand operated, seen on the left in the Up position, used as a permanent footbridge. Its replacement (*right*) was electrically operated. Beyond the canal, the single line split into Up and Down lines to pass under the SER main line viaduct towards Deptford Wharf. Lift Bridge signal box was an early Saxby pattern. *A.E.Bennett, The Transport Treasury, 1959*

Opposite bottom: The 'Thames Sider Special' rail tour was served by class M7 tank No 30050 and push-pull set No 717 of LBSCR stock. The rear coach is on the start of the spur to Old Kent Road. The timber yard is reminiscent of *The Plank*, a 1967 film starring Eric Sykes and Tommy Cooper (highly recommended if you have a wicked sense of humour). In the background the cranes of Deptford Wharf are visible in the background. *John J. Smith, Bluebell Railway Archives, 1959*

More from Alan in future issues, including Bricklayers Arms, Glastonbury, and Oxted.

Stephen Townroe's Colour Archive; the products of Mr Maunsell (mostly)

For this issue's instalment from the S. C. Townroe archive we have taken as our theme the products of Mr Maunsell (mostly) with a brief addition of the work of Mr Urie. (Next time the plan is for the Adams and Drummond classes to be featured.)

Above: In May 1951, No 30851 *Sir Francis Drake* is recorded at Southampton Central. Unfortunately we have not been able to ascertain the duty on this occasion. The '273' on the route disc – the latter for Bournemouth line services – is only something we have details on for 1954 by which time it was a BR Standard Class 4 Portsmouth - Salisbury turn avoiding Southampton. The presence of the tail lamp could well indicate the engine has even come off a train here and is in the siding before running light back to Eastleigh – after a boat train even?

Opposite top: Pre-Nationalisation days at Woking. No 855 *Robert Blake* setting off to head west on the fast line which at that time was not electrified. Workaday grime prevails; engine cleaning not perhaps always what we might think it might have been pre-1939.

Opposite bottom: Royal train duty for No 30864 *Sir Martin Frobisher* in Southampton Docks; no date but very early BR days as witness the wording on the tender and apple green livery – malachite was surely better. Last minute preparations are in hand with presumably the inspector standing alongside the driver.

Opposite: A sea of heads can be seen back from the engine as No 30862 *Lord Rodney* waits at Medstead and Four Marks station whilst in charge of an Up troop special. The delay is caused by the ordinary Alton – Southampton pull-push service occupying the single line from Alton hence the signalman waiting to receive the tablet which he will then put through his machine before withdrawing the same tablet again to give to the driver of No 30862, allowing it to proceed. Troop trains were rarely timed at particularly fast point to point timings whilst for No 30862 the hard work of the climb to the station is done and it is all downhill to Alton. May 1957. (With apologies for the black blemish of the left hand side.)

Opposite top: Doyen of the King Arthur class designed by Robert Urie and introduced from Eastleigh in 1918. This is No 30736 *King Arthur* at Bournemouth in 1949, the BR number applied in shaded lettering similar to the former ownership details on the tender. Some effort has been made to maintain a degree of cleanliness to tender and cabside and we can be certain there is also some green under the grime of the boiler.

Opposite bottom: The King Arthur class design was perpetuated by Maunsell from 1926 onwards but with detail differences – look at the cab roof for example. This too is how they could look when properly cleaned, No 30774 *Sir Gaheris* again in a mix of SR and BR livery at Eastleigh probably around 1949. The green smoke deflector paint was not continued in later years.

The final shade of green for the class, shown here on No 30783 *Sir Gillemere* at Eastleigh in 1949. The engine appears to be being serviced at both ends; smokebox cleaning and coaling but using a diesel crane. The crane is also on the site of the usual coal stack.

Top: Unidentified member of the class (Urie variant) 'somewhere' between Pirbright and Basingstoke with a holiday relief.

Bottom: This time it is passenger work for the freight variant of the 'KA' class: the S15. No 30522 entering Southampton Central from the west in April 1951. The two discs, one above each buffer, would imply a through service to the Western Region at Oxford from Bournemouth West, in which case an S15 was an unusual choice for this type of train. Not perhaps of the best technically with the colours unfortunately starting to deteriorate.

Opposite top: Another engine type going back some years was this time H15 4-6-0 No 30474 undergoing valve setting as one of the last stages of its overhaul at Eastleigh in 1951. No 30474 would remain active until the end of April 1960.

Opposite bottom: 'The best 4-4-0 in the country….'; that is almost certainly what SCT would have said for as we know he was a proponent of the Maunsell designs as being predictable and reliable. It was genuinely unfortunate when the survivors of the Schools class were written off – literally with the stroke of a pen – on 31 December 1962. Several could have lasted longer but the demise of steam was accelerating and fewer classes meant fewer spares and consequently savings in costs. In better BR days, No 30911 *Dover* is seen near to Petts Wood in September 1954.

This page, top: Most would agree the Schools looked better in green; subjective as to whether this was the Southern or BR(S) variant. In the former category we see a work stained No 922 *Marlborough* at Eastleigh amidst the piles of detritus associated with the steam railway c1948/49.

This page, bottom: Another BR liveried black engine, No 30921 at London Bridge on what is either an Eastbourne or Hastings service.

Mr Maunsell was also responsible for two large tank engine designs intended for freight and shunting. One was the 'W' class of 2-6-4T, built using parts salvaged from the River class when these were turned into tender engines. The W type were often to be found working cross-London freight turns or transfer services between the various Southern yards. Here No 31913 is performing this type of working probably early in BR days and without any evidence of ownership.

Finally for this issue one of the chunky members of the Z type 0-8-0T, No 30956, believed to be near to Totton. Z class engines were to be found at Eastleigh and Exmouth Junction, at the latter location used primarily for banking from Exeter St Davids to Exeter Central.

Riding the 'Rivers'

It has been commonplace in recent years to deride the 2-6-4T design River tanks and not unnaturally this is based upon the Sevenoaks accident of 1927.

We should not forget however several points. Firstly the LBSCR had in service some even larger 4-6-4T engines, seven of these built between 1914 and 1922. It also made sense to use a tank engine on a limited length service where platform occupancy was consequently less than a locomotive with separate tender. In theory the tank engine had only to run round its train ready for the return working (servicing excluded), although it will be noted that few – if any – images have come to light showing bunker first working on a fast service with the inevitable conclusion that crews still preferred to run with the chimney facing forward, hence any time that might have been saved through not using a turntable at the destination was negated. Large tank engines were also in use on passenger working elsewhere, including on the Furness Railway, whilst the third of the SR constituents, the LSWR, had on their books the five members of the Urie 4-6-2T class although it must be admitted these were intended for, and indeed used for, work other than passenger services. (We are deliberately leaving out of the equation the use of 2-6-4T and 2-6-2T designs on suburban and outer suburban services as was the case later on the LNER, LMS, GWR, and of course BR.)

Harold Holcroft, in his biographical works 'Locomotive Adventure' Parts 1 & 2 (1963 and 1965 respectively), both Ian Allan, recounts his experiences with No 790 of the 'K' (River) class in the years prior to Sevenoaks. Rather than repeat Holcroft verbatim, we may conveniently summarise that No 790 was comfortable to ride on and coped well with the loads it was given. It was also noted as having a roomy cab – something we will pick up upon again later. Holcroft made several footplate trips starting in December 1921 and continuing into January 1922. In all cases these were on ordinary service trains. Further trials this time involving an example of the 'L' and 'D1', both 4-4-0 classes of tender engines, took place in the autumn of 1922, the 'K' reported as being the most economical of the three. It was on the basis of these trials and the performance of No 790 that the order was placed in 1923 for a further 20 engines of the 'K' class to be built.

The important point to make at this stage being there was no report of any rolling or harsh riding.

Post-Sevenoaks

Following the Sevenoaks accident riding trials were carried out with examples of the 'K' and 'K1' class on the LNER and SR. As to why the LNER was selected is not explained. But equally if it had been the GWR we might now be asking why not the LNER? It would probably be fair to conclude the LMS main line was simply too congested.

Appendix V1 to the MoT accident report on Sevenoaks quotes:

Mr Gresley's report on Trials with Southern Railway Company's Tank and Tender Engines addressed to the Inspecting Officers enquiries stated:

'Dear Sir,

'In accordance with your request, I have carried out a series of running trials at high speed with Tank and Tender engines of the Southern Railway.

'These trials were made on 16 October between Huntingdon and St Neots on the Great Northern section of the London and North Eastern Railway main line and were repeated on 30 October between Woking and Walton on the Western Section main line of the Southern Railway.

'The engines used in both series of trials were

1 – No 803 2-6-4 tank engine (2 cylinders)
2 - No 890 2-6-4 tank engine (3 cylinders)
3 – No 782 4-6-0 tender engine (2 cylinders)

'In order to attain quickly a high rate of speed on the trial runs, only two carriages were attached to the engine, one of these being a Dynamometer Car for accurately recording the speeds during the trials. *(Note – other than necessary dynamometer car connections, although as steaming and efficiency was not being tested and it was instead just a speed assessment and riding qualities, no mention is made of the engines having been especially prepared for the tests – Ed.)*

'On all the trials I rode on the footplate to instruct the drivers as to the speeds and observe the oscillation and general behaviour of the engines. Mr Moore of the Ministry of Transport also rode on the footplate. In addition, two of my staff were on the footplate taking records with a portable Accelerometer made by the Cambridge Instrument Company, which recorded the vertical and lateral accelerations of the engines.

'The weather conditions during the trials were similar, being fine and clear, and the same drivers were employed on both occasions.'

No of Trial	Engine	Direction of Running	Road	Condition of Tanks and Bunkers	Speeds	Observations
Trials with Southern Railway Engines on London and North Eastern Railway 16 October 1927.						
Tank Engines Nos 803, 890						
1	803	Forwards	Up	Nearly empty	67¼ - 73¼	Engine ran without roll or lateral motion on straight and curves except for a slight roll at about 55¾ mile post and again a lesser roll at 54¾ mile post.
2	803	Backwards	Down	Nearly empty	67 - 73½	Engine ran quite smoothly and without any rolling or lurching.
3	890	Forwards	Up	Nearly empty	73½ - 77	Engine rather more lively on its springs than 803 and not quite so steady. A slight roll was noticeable at 55¾ mile post and at 54¾ mile post, otherwise she ran smoothly and did not roll.
4	890	Backwards	Down	Nearly empty	77½ - 83¼	A very satisfactory trial, engine ran, if anything, steadier than 803, bunker first, and there was no rolling nor lurching although 83¼ mph was attained.
5	803	Forwards	Up	Full	72½ - 78	Engine ran steadier than when empty on No 1 trip. In fact considering speed, it could be regarded as being on this trip a very steady, comfortably engine.
6	803	Backwards	Down	Full	68 - 77½	Running of engine very steady and smooth throughout trip.
7	890	Forwards	Up	Full	74 - 77½	Not quite so steady as engine 803, Trip 5, but better than when running with tanks and bunkers empty on Trip 3.
8	890	Backwards	Down	Full	69¾ - 78	Engine ran very steadily.
9	803	Forwards	Up	Three-quarters full	56¾ - 59¾	These trials at reduced speeds were carried out at the suggestion of the Chief Engineer of the Southern Railway with a view to learning whether, at lower speeds, any periodical oscillation might be set up. The engines ran quite steadily and without any undue oscillation.
10	803	Backwards	Down	Three-quarters full	62¼ - 66¼	
11	890	Forwards	Up	Nearly empty	61½ - 68¾	
12	890	Backwards	Down	Nearly empty	57½ - 64¾	
Tender Engine No 782						
13	782	Forwards	Up	Ordinary running conditions	75 - 81½	The engine ran with perfect steadiness without any roll or lurch, but the vibration on the footplate was so great that it was impossible to obtain any record with the Accelerometer.

No 803 *River Itchen* seen receiving last minute driver attention. This was one of the engines involved in the trials on both the LNER and SR subsequent to Sevenoaks. Earlier in the text mention was made of Holcroft's comment that the class had a '…roomy cab.' They needed one too; on the LNER trials those present were the SR driver, SR fireman, an LNER pilotman – as the Southern crew would certainly not have known the road - Mr Gresley, Mr Moore from the Ministry of Transport and two members of Mr Gresley's staff – at least seven persons. If Mr Ellson the SR Chief Engineer was also present this would have made matters even more cramped and even more difficult for the fireman who would have needed to keep the firebox fed in order to maintain the necessary pressure to achieve the speeds recorded. A similar number would have been likewise present on the Southern. *Rail Archive Stephenson*

The unique 3-cylinder engine, No 890 *River Frome,* which was also involved in the trials. The divided drive with the link from the crosshead passing in front of the outside cylinder valve chest was initially common with the three cylinder Maunsell tender engines and had been a Holcroft design. It was later altered due to excess wear occurring. *Rail Archive Stephenson*

Trials with Southern Railway Engines on Southern Railway 30 October 1927.

No of Trial	Engine	Direction of Running	Road	Condition of Tanks and Bunkers	Speeds	Observations
Tank Engines Nos 803, 890						
1	803	Forwards	Up	Nearly empty	44½ - 63	Only moderate speed was attempted on this run, engine rolled slightly at several points and was not so steady as on L&NE
2	803	Backwards	Down	Nearly empty	34¼ - 69¼	Only moderate speed was attempted. Engine rode steadier than in No 1 trip. Down road appeared to be in better condition than Up road.
3	890	Forwards	Up	Nearly empty	51½ - 77¾	Engine rolled at several points but quickly recovered itself, five oscillations being the greatest number occurring together in quick succession. These oscillations or rolls were the worst experienced in any of the trials. Some were on the straight road, others on entering curves, and again where superelevation of outer rails changed. I did not regard the roll as particularly dangerous, but if it had increased instead of abated, should have promptly applied the brake.
4	890	Backwards	Down	Nearly empty	31 - 69¾	Engine rode much better than on Up road, the speed was lower than in preceding run, and the road in better condition. There was a slight roll at the 19¼ mile post.
5	803	Forwards	Up	Full	50 - 77½	The engine rolled to about the same extent as engine 890 on Trip 3 and at the same point.
6	803	Backwards	Down	Full	31 - 73½	Engine ran fairly steadily and better than when empty.
7	890	Forwards	Up	Full	52 - 68	Speed reduced on this trip owing to instructions (?) received from Chief Engineer, but rolling still considerable at bad points.
8	890	Backwards	Down	Full	33½ - 70	Engine running was fairly satisfactory and seemed rather better than on Trial 4 when empty. There were some vertical oscillations but no rolling to speak of. (Sir John Pringle rode on footplate.)
Tender Engine No 782						
9	782	Forwards	Up	Ordinary running conditions	66¾ - 86	The vibration was, if anything, worse than on the London and North Eastern. At the places where rolling occurred with the Tank engines, there was considerable rolling and lurching with the tender engine, and the riding can be described as very rough and uncomfortable.

No 790 *River Avon* on the Brighton line at the head of nine Pullmans. From Clapper we learn that there were bad patches of track on the Brighton line, repairs to which had been shelved due to cost. Sevenoaks might then almost have been an accident waiting to happen with no one realising the deteriorating state of the track at several places. Consequently it would be unfair to place all the blame on the River class engines as the principal cause. *Rail Archive Stephenson*

'General Conclusions.

'There is little difference between the running of the two tank engines. Compared with the Tender engine they ride more softly and more comfortably. When on a bad patch of road the period of the roll of the Tank engines is longer and easier but, I think, of greater amplitude. The Tender engine has stiffer springs, consequently rides more **rigidity** and the roll is shorter. I should expect the running of the Tender engine would be more detrimental to the road at high speeds than that of the Tank engines.

'The two-cylinder engine No 803 is slightly steadier than the three-cylinder No 890, probably because No 803 has laminated springs on the pony truck and bogie, whereas on No 890 helical springs are used. The coupled wheel springs are similar on both engines, the leading and trailing coupled wheels have laminated springs and the centre coupled wheels helical. I think engine 890 would probably ride as well as 803 if the laminated springs were fitted to the pony truck

and bogie. In other respects 890 is the better engine of the two.

'When running backwards, bunker first, with the bogies leading, the riding of both Tank engines was distinctly steadier than when running forwards with the pony truck leading.

'Both engines ran noticeably steadier when water tanks and coal bunkers were full than when they were practically empty.

'There is a marked difference in the conditions of the sections of track of the London and North Eastern and Southern railways over which the trial runs were made.

'Both the Tank and Tender engines ran with remarkable steadiness at high speeds on the London and North Eastern track. The curves are all transition curves and the general conditions of the road were superior to that of the Southern. I am satisfied that on the London and North Eastern section of the road over which the trials were made, both Tank and

Opposite side view of the 2-cylinder No 792 *River Arun* at Brighton. With the exception of the GWR – we might say who were always different – the 2-6-4T wheel arrangement became standard for large passenger tank engines in the last decades of steam, as witness the LNER Thompson type as well as the designs of the LMS and BR. Several of the parts for the River design, the largest probably the rear bogies, were subsequently used in the new 'W' class 2-6-4T design; but these were *NEVER* used on any passenger service. *Rail Archive Stephenson*

Tender engines could run regularly with safety at any speed which they could attain.

'On the trial portion of the Southern Railway the rolling of both Tank and Tender engines was excessive at high speeds; the rolling of the engines at some places when running on the straight line was quite as great as the worst roll experienced on curves.

'It seemed clear to me that this rolling was caused by irregular depression of the road at various points, apparently owing to the sleepers not being properly packed, and to defective drainage.

'The rolling of both Tank and Tender engines at speeds of 70mph is greater than I consider safe for regular working on roads in a condition similar to that of the Southern Railway over which the trials were made.

'If the location of the irregular depressions in the road previously referred to should coincide with the rolling periods of engines, a dangerous and unstable condition would arise.

As it is not so likely that such irregularities would occur as close to each other as to coincide with the shorter rolling periods of Tender engines, there is less probability of this dangerous condition arising with Tender engines than with Tank engines.

'Both the Tank engines are well designed efficient engines, and on a road well laid and well maintained are suitable for working express passenger trains.'

Signed H. N. Gresley.'

A further report '…impressions…' by Mr J. L. M. Moore * of the Ministry of Transport was also appended,

'In respect of the London and North Eastern Railway section, the steadiness of the tank engines was particularly noticeable throughout, and on no occasion was anything in the nature of a continuous roll set up. The directional changes in curvature were negotiated more smoothly on the trial runs when the tank engine was running bunker first, ie with the bogie wheels leading, than in the opposite direction, when there was a tendency at first to lurch. The engines appeared to be rather steadier when travelling with side tanks full, and No 803 (2 cylinder) was less susceptible to irregularities in the track than No 890 (3 cylinder).

'As regards the trial runs with tender engine No 782 ('King Arthur' class), there was smooth running with little oscillation noticeably on the first trial when the maximum speed of 72 miles an hour was attained. On the second trial when the speed of 82mph was reached, slight but steady rolling was set up on two occasions but the effect of the variations in curvature were hardly noticeable. Vibration of the footplate was more pronounced than in the case of either of the tank engines.

'On the Southern Railway section, the tank engine did not run so steadily, and distinct periods of oscillation of hot duration were experienced when travelling on the Up main line – more or less at the same place on each run. As there were no directional changes of curvature to account for them, we thought the movements were probably the result of imperfections in the permanent way. On the Down track the rolling movement was less noticeable, which suggested that the track might be in better condition, though the improvement might possibly have been due again to the fact that the bogie of the tank engine was at the front. Engine 890 again appeared to be slightly less steady than No 803. On one occasion when travelling with the former (tanks full) on the Up line, a slight jar was felt giving the impression that the framing of the engine had come in contact with the tops of the axle boxes on one side during a roll.

'On the one trial made with engine No 782, when a maximum speed of about 86mph was attained, a certain amount of oscillation was experienced, such as might be expected on any engine travelling at so high a speed, and several rather pronounced shock rolls occurred at the same points on the Up line, very similar in degree to those experienced on the tank engines. Vibration was again very marked, suggesting that the springing of the engine was somewhat harsh.'

Mr Moore concluded that he did not consider that any of the engines showed any marked tendency to roll continuously. When their steadiness was disturbed by imperfections in the track, or other causes, the oscillation was neither excessive in his view nor of long duration. The rapidity with which the engine settled down after rolling was noticeable.

In view of the greater number of trials made with the tank engines he found it difficult to draw a fair comparison of their movement with the tender engine. There appeared to be very little difference between the three engines with regard to rolling movements when they were travelling with the bogie wheels leading. In the other direction the tank engines were slightly less steady, and more inclined to lurch and develop rolling movement when encountering directional changes of curvature. The greater 'liveliness' which was shown by engine No 890 as compared with No 803 he thought was probably due to the springing arrangements between the two engines.

So why if it was almost certain the poor condition of the track on the Southern was to blame did Walker go to the bother and expense on the SR of instructing the class be rebuilt as tender engines? Surely they could have been found less speed-related work thereby saving the costs involved? It also goes to show just how much influence and control Walker wielded so far as his heads of departments were concerned. Even so the work both in reballasting and rebuilding would have had to be approved by the directors but they were clearly content to take the advice of their General Manager.

Possibly the answer is that Walker was possibly erring on the side of safety and public and possibly staff opinion as well. Would the K class ever be trusted again even if restricted to a lower speed by dictat? There could be no guarantee an engine crew might not one day feel compelled to resort to higher speeds when delayed through no fault of their own especially as the class were not fitted with speedometers.

More significant perhaps was that it was clear the SR p/way was nowhere up to the standard of that on the LNER and this in itself was the responsibility of the Chief Engineer. Even so we should not be unduly hard on Ellson. His area of responsibility was vast, no doubt he was attempting to ensure all was well throughout the system and it was an impossible task. We should also not forget his resources were likely spread thinly on the ground and although not stated it may well have been that with the various electrification schemes being worked upon, staff had been purloined to work on these compared with general maintenance. The damage caused by 'modern' motive power to track not always in the best condition seems not to have been fully understood back in 1927, but it was a lesson evidently not recalled 40 years later, as witness Hither Green in 1967.

Referring again to Holcroft, it was Walker who wanted to have the LNER trials repeated on the Western Section of the SR main line, '...which was considered to be superior construction to that of the Eastern...... when Gresley called them off before attempting high speed, as the riding at 70mph was not good enough and it was considered unsafe to proceed; this disillusionment was quite a shock to the GM '.

Charles Clapper comments that it was also Gilbert Szlumper (then the Assistant General Manager of the SR) who had given orders on the evening of the accident at Sevenoaks for the whole of the River class of engines to remain on shed. (Sir) John Elliot subsequently confirmed this in his own biography (Allen & Unwin):

'On August 24 1927, one of Maunsell's two-cylinder 2-6-4 tank engines left the track with a Down express on leaving Polhill Tunnel and 13 passengers in all lost their lives. This followed three other incidents on the Eastern Section with this type of engine. Gilbert Szlumper gave immediate orders that evening for the classes ('plural' as he was referring to the K and K1 type of tank engine; two and three cylinder designs) to remain on shed until an

investigation had been made. Sir John Elliot, who was present at a meeting in Walker's room very soon afterwards, stated in 'The Journal of Transport History', that Maunsell maintained that the engine was perfectly stable at any speed on a good track, and George Ellson, the chief engineer, who had succeeded Szlumper senior (as Chief Engineer) only a few weeks before, was equally certain that his track was not the cause. Walker's action was immediate and characteristic. He neither accepted nor rejected the conflicting opinions and after asking a number of questions which showed that the difference in opinion was fundamental, he reflected for a minute or two and then said in a quiet voice: 'A number of people have lost their lives on our railway, so there must be something wrong somewhere. Maunsell, we will withdraw the whole of this class of locomotives from traffic for the time being, and it may be wise to convert them into tender engines. Let me have the cost.

'Ellson, please prepare for me for the next board meeting your estimate of the cost of re-ballasting the whole of the boat train route between London and Dover......' W. A. Willox, who was assistant divisional engineer on the Eastern Division at the time and later the chief assistant editor of The Railway Gazette confirmed that, already alarmed by the running of the K class tank engines on the Central Section, he had marked out bad spots in his division and prepared a programme of improvement but which had been shelved by his superior as too costly to recommend. Both the Brighton and South Eastern administrations had a policy of shingle ballast on ash foundations and the King Arthur engines and heavier coaches had begun to knock the permanent way about. The subsequent reballasting was done with Meldon stone and soft spots were blanketed to stop the track pumping up and down with passing trains.

'A non-technical general manager had succeeded in making two decisions on the right lines soon after an incident that might

No 782 *Sir Brian*; the engine used on the comparative trials, passing Raynes Park with a Down West of England train. Raynes Park is just a few miles east of where the SR trials took place; between Woking and Walton. *The Transport Treasury*

forgivably have otherwise aroused merely emotional reactions.

'For the board regret was expressed at the accident, of which particulars were given by Walker. Remuneration for the doctors concerned was authorised to be given through the solicitor and a tribute was paid to the ready assistance on the scene of the company's men trained in ambulance work. Later a donation of twice the recorded treatment costs was made to Sevenoaks & Holmesdale Hospital, with warm thanks.'

It remains a matter of regret that no illustrations of the trials on either the LNER or SR have seemingly ever appeared. Perhaps it was simply that they were kept quiet.

☐ According to 'Steam Index' Mr J. L. M. Moore was a civilian inspector working for the Board of Trade between 1929 and 1953 – clearly prior to the earlier date as well. In 1942 he had gained the title Director General, Ministry of War Transport in report on the Brighton accident in which 14 soldiers were killed. (The 'Brighton' referred to was on the LNER Nottingham to Sheffield line.) The incident having taken place on 11 February 1942 when a northbound troop train struck a heavy steel plate on a stationary wagon in Holbrook Colliery Sidings. The steel plate penetrated some of the coaches carrying 400 naval or military persons. A total of 14 soldiers were killed and 35 were seriously injured. Mr. Moore deprecated the lack of secure means for retaining the plate.

From the archives: Southern Signal Boxes
Part 2 Some Power Box exteriors

Continuing on from Issue 2, we are delighted to offer a number of power box exterior views. Power boxes by their very nature would invariably take over the work of several former manual boxes in the area, operation varying from 'one lever – one movement' through to route setting and remote operation over a wide area.

The advantages were obvious, less mechanical wear and tear, knowledge and control of operation over a wide area and of course a saving in staffing costs. But there were other costs to consider as well, not always financial. Men made redundant from closed boxes or reduced to pushing a broom on a platform if their application for the limited number of posts available in the new location was unsuccessful. Perhaps the greatest weakness was should a failure occur then the knock-on effect might well affect services over a wide radius. Progress yes, but with every advantage comes disadvantages; as all of us who have ever been affected by 'signalling delays' may well vouch for.

The new signal box at Cannon Street photographed on 15 December 1957 which had replaced the former 143 lever mechanical signal box destroyed by fire on 5 April 1967. The box opened the day after the photograph was taken replacing the second of two temporary signals boxes - the first of which had been in a brake van – but allowing restricted use of the station whilst the second temporary structure and then the new building, seen here, was completed and commissioned. *British Railways*

'New signal box, Hither Green', according to the official caption, photographed on 26 January 1962. Remote electric control over a wide area but as will also be noted for the time, good observation from the operating floor. The visibility issue was a carry-over from mechanical days when the signalman was expected to observe trains as they pass, 'to check for the presence of a tail lamp and to observe for any signs of distress or concern'. British Railways

Southern Railway 'Glasshouse' type signal box at Horsham. Opened on 24 April 1938, we are perhaps bending the rules slightly to refer to this as a power frame as inside was a Westinghouse A2 frame of 90 levers. Our justification is that not all the signals / points here were mechanically operated. In the background is the water tower for the engine shed whilst the ground floor ends were taken up with stores and workshops. Horsham was operational until 27 August 2005. British Railways

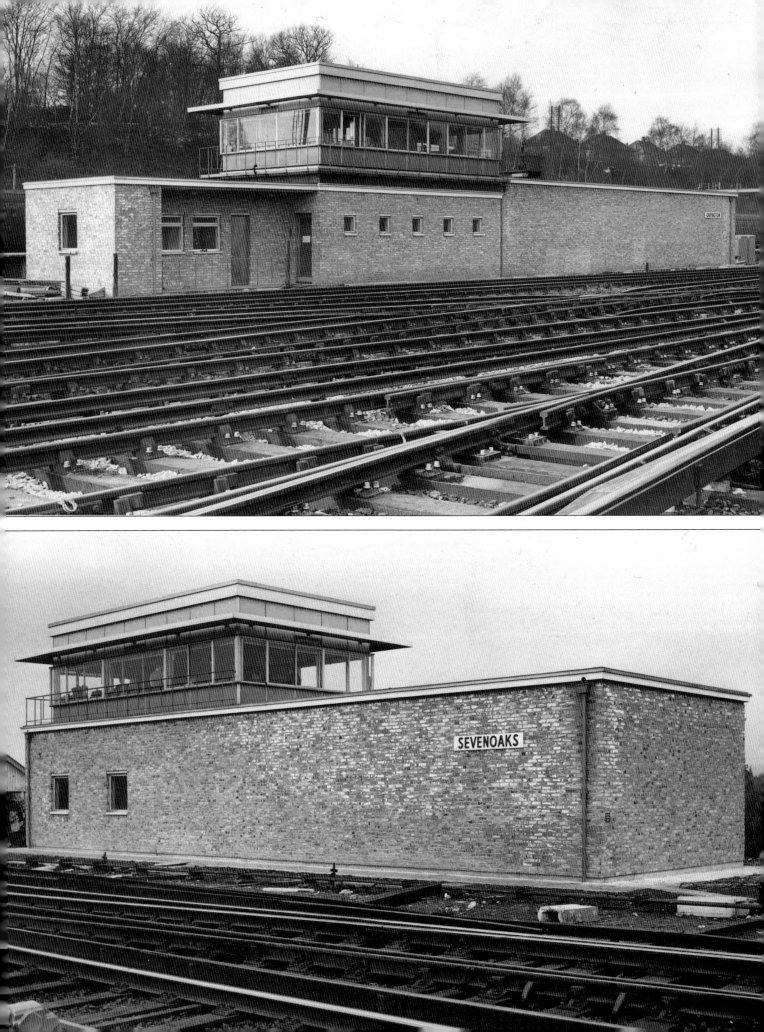

Opposite top: The new signal box at Orpington on 5 March 1962, the day after commissioning. This was a true power box with an NX panel fitted – true route setting; the signalman (contemporary designation) would press a button where the approaching train entered his field of control and a second button where he wished it to exit. The system checking the route, changing points and engaging locks as necessary with the clearing of the signals the last phase. The same buttons might well be used in the opposite aspect if a train were travelling over an identical line but approaching from the opposite direction – obviously not at the same time and assuming bi-direction working was permitted. Orpington closed 31 years later on 22 March 1993. *British Railways*

Opposite bottom: A similar NX panel was installed at Sevenoaks when that too opened on 4 March 1962. We deliberately use the term similar – it could not be identical as the track layouts at Orpington and Sevenoaks were of necessity different. Observation balcony around the outside and some shading to the windows in both cases. Even so, signal boxes were often hot-houses in consequence of the large amount of glass present. The contrasting colours of the brickwork used was a pleasing touch. *British Railways*

Above: The new structure at Shepherds Lane just beyond Clapham on the lines from Victoria. This was the fourth box with the name 'Shepherds Lane / Shepherds Lane Junction' and was in use from 8 March 1959 until 29 November 1981. A modern derivative perhaps of the much older LSWR 'centre pillar' design, inside were 23 levers working a Westinghouse A2 frame. With no obvious outlets for point or signal wiring, it is reasonable to assume all were in effect little more than electric switches controlled by short levers. *British Railways*

Above: Also a 'day after opening' view, Shortlands Junction taken on 31 May 1959 (by co-incidence this caption is being compiled on the same day 63 years later). Another NX panel with an operational life of a few days over 23 years. The design is somewhat futuristic compared with what might well be described as the more traditional structures of before; not just rectangles but also note the tangential sides at the front. Even so far less offensive to the eye compared with something like Birmingham New Street 'signal centre' of a few years later – but then that is the LMR! *British Railways*

Opposite top: Another 'Glasshouse' box, the now listed Surbiton, the interior of which we saw in the previous issue. Very much 'art-deco' in style, its design complemented the rebuilding of the station here around the same time: 1936. *British Railways*

Opposite bottom: The uniquely designed Victoria Central box. Opened in June 1939, it replaced three other structures so concentrating operations at the one place. Inside were three separate lever frames each at an angle to the next and all consisting of Westinghouse L frames totalling 225 levers. The new Victoria Signalling Centre had replaced its operational use by 1981 but the structure remains, albeit no longer applied for signalling. *British Railways*

From the archives will continue in Issue 4 with Southern Publicity

The LSWR A12 class (The 'Jubilees')

Compared with the 35 members of the G6 class of 0-6-0T tank engines we looked at in the last issue, this time we are dealing with a class of 90 engines, still a six-wheel design but now a four coupled tender engine with a single carrying axle mounted at the rear in the form of an 0-4-2; the LSWR A12 design. Mounting a carrying axle within a rigid frame rather than at the front might seem a slightly strange idea, but not quite unique in 19th century locomotive design and had the added advantage of allowing more space for the firebox and ashpan at the rear. (The 2-4-0 tender type was however more commonplace as was the 0-4-2T tank design.)

The first ten engines of the A12 design appeared in the Golden Jubilee year of Queen Victoria, 1887, and consequently they took the unofficial title of the 'Jubilee' class; even so none bore names.

The A12 class had come about after a recognised need for what was in effect a mixed-traffic locomotive having a wide route availability. (This same requirement was the holy grail of so many designers in the steam age – including of course one 'Mr Bulleid', but I think we have said enough about Mr B's supposed choice for now!)

Thus it was that on 23 June 1886 the Locomotive Superintendent, Mr Adams, received permission to proceed with his new design, an 0-4-2 mixed traffic tender engine having a weight of just 42 tons and with it almost complete route availability. Twenty were ordered, to be built at Nine Elms at a cost of £1,630 each. Delivery commenced in May 1887 and the last of what was to be the first batch took to the rails in June 1888. They were given the numbers 527 through to 546. Thirty further engines were constructed at Nine Elms and another 40 by Neilson and Co., Nine Elms having insufficient capacity to complete the full batch. The final total was

90, the last entering service in May 1895. Number series was from 527 to 556 and 597 to 656. Order numbers were, 'A12', 'E1', 'M2', 'O4', and 'K6' although they were collectively referred to as 'A12' and of course 'Jubilees'.

Being built over an eight-year period there were various modifications made based on experience in traffic and also for varying requirements. These variations included tender type; 1,950 to 3,300 gallon water capacity, reversing; screw / pole, cylinder valve position, chimneys, braking vacuum or vacuum plus Westinghouse, blast pipe dimensions, and weight distribution.

The class were popular and well used for the type of traffic intended, the Westinghouse fitted engines finding employment on through workings to and from the SECR and LBSCR systems, consequently these engines were based at Nine Elms, Strawberry Hill, Guildford and Fratton. Otherwise they might be seen working anywhere on the South Western system and were often preferred by drivers to one of the newer Drummond 4-4-0 types; the latter more coal hungry and consequently affecting the pay packet of the drivers of the day who were paid a coal bonus based on how little fuel they might use.

Bradley reports but without detailed elaboration, how soon into 1915 '...refrigerated meat van trains...' started to run from the ports of Liverpool and Bristol destined for shipment to the Western Front Supply Depots. These would require an engine change at Salisbury, Basingstoke and Willesden, the last named often routed via Alton so as to avoid congestion on the main line. What is not stated is how such a '....heavy....' train might thus have fared 'Over the Alps' - the steep gradient south of Alton as far as Medstead and Four Marks.

The class was intact at the time of the Southern Railway takeover in 1923 and all

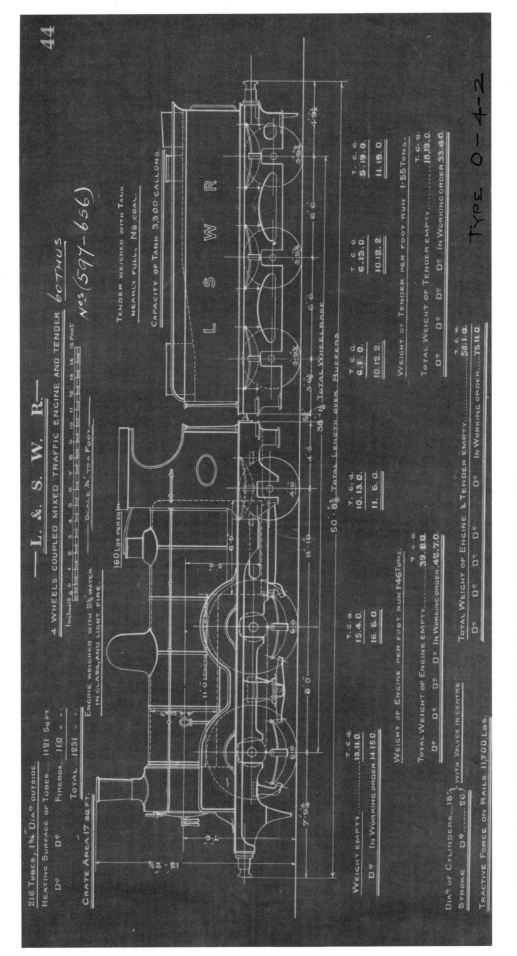

Official drawing of 'A12' (Order No 'O4'), Nos 597 to 656, built from 1893

No 655 of the same batch as the drawing attached to a 3,300 gallon capacity tender. Coal capacity was not stated. Engine and tender fully lined. Fluted coupling rods, and for its time, reasonable cab roof protection for the crew.

were eventually repainted in the plain Southern livery, a number of the class having already lost their decorative brass beading by this time although others went through their whole live with this embellishment intact. Repainted engines were originally fitted with the 'E' (Eastleigh) prefix but this started to disappear after 1931. Drummond pattern boilers also started to appear from 1925 onwards.

The class remained intact until 1928 when six engines ceased work. After this there were sporadic withdrawals every year through to 1939. Additionally in April 1932 an edict had been issued prohibiting further major repairs. Fortunately Eastleigh retained a good supply of spares including five copper fireboxes and six sets of cylinders. Spare parts did not however run to items such as sets of frames and six engines, Nos 551, 607, 608, 610, 653 and 656, succumbed in 1932 due to frame, crank axles and tyre

issues and very likely other defects in addition.

Bradley also provides us with some details as to the types of work being performed by the class members based at Eastleigh in the 1930s involved in local goods and passenger turns to Lymington, Wimborne, Hamworthy Junction, Dorchester, Fawley, Southampton, Gosport, Romsey, Andover, Winchester and Winchester (Cheesehill) and Alton. Co-incidentally the Maunsell 'Q' class design of 1938 not only took the same numbers 530 to 549 from by now withdrawn 'A12s' but also took over similar and sometimes even the same duties.

Seven more engines were withdrawn in 1939 but were stored rather than

being scrapped, six subsequently reinstated into general service, the seventh, No 646, had been diagnosed with cracked frames and was instead taken to Salisbury where it was used to supply steam to the new 'Merchant Navy' class

Top: Doyen of the class, No 527, seen at Nine Elms with the full LSWR initials on the tender. Right-hand drive, as witness the link to the weigh shaft leading down from the cab. Fully lined livery and it will be noted the sandbox is included in the splasher of the front driving wheel. Transport Treasury

Bottom: This time we see No 616, one of the 40 of the class built by Neilson & Co. to their works numbers 4506 through to 4545. Safety chains are fitted and there is a reasonable width platform on the front framing for emptying the smokebox. Maker's plate affixed to the splasher above the second driving wheel. Transport Treasury

Cab view of No 632, another Neilson & Co. build, from January 1893. The forty engines erected by this company arrived on the LSWR over an 18 month period between November 1892 and April 1893. This engine can be seen to have a lever (pole) reverser fitted. It survived until August 1937.

No 609. As with most of the accompanying images, no dates are given but what may be noted is the standard of cleanliness that was applied even to mixed traffic engines. The hook on the side of the tender towards the front was for carrying a spare headcode disc. This engine was in service from November 1892 to April 1947.

No 631, undated and clearly hauling GWR stock. The location is not given whilst the head code of two discs does not appear to apply to any obvious duty where the GWR might be involved – comments from readers would be appreciated. All we can say for certain is Southern livery and sometime prior to withdrawal in June 1933. Bradley refers to the class as being the 'Mogul' type equivalent of their day. *Transport Treasury*

engines so as to keep these ready for almost continuous service.

Despite their clearly limited remaining life, two, Nos 638 and 600, even managed to acquire Bulleid malachite green livery with cabside numerals, others repainted around this time were in unlined Maunsell green with the more usual pattern of tender numerals. Subsequent repainting of any engine was in plain black from April 1941 onwards.

Between January 1942 and February 1944 five of the class were transferred away from the Southern for home military use at Longmoor and Melbourne. A sixth engine, No 645, had also left the Southern at the

same time but subsequently found its way to Kineton and later Bicester. From the latter No 645 was seen working weekend leave trains to Oxford until it too returned to the Southern in April 1945. Nos 614 and 618 even managed to receive repairs at Derby during their 'away time'.

Of the 31 engines that had been on the books in 1939 – this excludes the 'steaming' engine No 646 at Salisbury - 30 survived through to the end of war in Europe. The exception was No 555 which had in early 1942 also been given the alternative number 3555 on the basis that the then new 'Q1' class were to be numbered from 555 onwards. As we know, the 'Q1' type instead took the numbers C1

Left: No 641 working a goods train over a third rail section and possibly near Feltham; again location assistance is welcome. We have deliberately included this and the previous view for whilst not of the best quality they do show examples of the class other than in a static environment. In the years immediately prior to WW1 the class were averaging just over 35,000 miles annually, a respectable figure for a type often restricted to local services. *Transport Treasury*

Bottom: No 535 of the first series awaiting repair at Nine Elms following an altercation – we might wonder what the other party looked like! With the front end part dismantled there is also a good view of the right hand cylinder (18in diameter). The late Barry Curl, in his book 'The LSWR at Nine Elms Part 1' (KRB Publications 2004), comments on p197 that the class appeared prone to accidents. This is possibly a bit unfair and may well be based simply on the existence of several accident type views. Even so Bradley gives details of two accidents involving class members Nos 532 and 556. The former was in charge of a goods train at Wimborne on 29 November 1894 with the driver attempting to make up time. Unfortunately such exuberance resulted in him approaching the home signal too fast and he was then unable to stop before colliding with the rear of a workmans' train. Only minor damage was caused and the engine was later able to continue on its booked turn with a goods from Dorchester. Sister engine No 556 had been involved in a collision involving a 17 coach passenger train of air-braked LBSCR stock at Hampton Court on 20 June 1890. In this case it was down to the driver attempting to place as much of his train as possible under the shelter of the platform canopy on a wet day. This meant he would have to stop close to the buffers and he simply misjudged his braking and the operation of the Westinghouse brake. *Curl Collection*

No 618 at Guildford. In the latter part of WW1 and possibly into Southern days, Guildford had an allocation of 25 of the class engaged on Waterloo semi-fast turns, plus local goods and troop and munitions services from Aldershot as far as Redhill where a changeover was made with the SECR. Livery perhaps not quite as clean as in earlier years. At the rear of the engine is a Mogul yet to receive smoke deflectors. *Transport Treasury*

through to C40 and No 3555 reverted to its original identification after just a few days. No 555 was withdrawn from Guildford in February 1944 having achieved a recorded 1,218,149 miles in a lifetime of just over 54 years.

Notwithstanding a return to peace it might have been expected that the survivors would almost immediately succumb but not quite so. It could hardly have been said they were in the best of condition but then neither was much else of the fleet and so just one, No 641, went in 1945 but was followed by 12 in 1946. A further 18 went in 1947 so leaving just four out of the original 90 strong class to pass into the hands of British Railways.

None of these four were repainted or renumbered, the last of the four withdrawn on 20 November 1948 after having spent its final duty shunting Town yard. Together

with sister No 627, also withdrawn in 1948, the pair were broken up at Eastleigh in January 1949.

One of the 1946 withdrawals from traffic however still remained, the former No 612 taken out of traffic in June 1946 but which had been renumbered in the service stock list as DS5319 and was kept employed supplying steam to the Eastleigh boiler yard until finally scrapped in November 1951. These of course were the days before anything like major strides had been made in the preservation field and consequently none survive.

Reference:

'LSWR Locomotives: The Adams Classes' by D. L. Bradley. Published Wild Swan 1985.

With grateful thanks also to Ian Wilkins.

Top: No 555 at Guildford, 12 March 1938. This was the engine temporarily renumbered 3555 in 1942 and also the only member of the class to be taken out of service during WW2. It had been one of six of the class at the time fitted with the Westinghouse air brake in addition to vacuum equipment. When so fitted the pump was attached to the right hand side of the firebox and the air reservoir below the frames between the rear-most driving wheel and the carrying axle. The Westinghouse equipment was removed from the so fitted engines between 1912 and 1931; two, Nos 538 and 543, were withdrawn with the fittings still present. *Transport Treasury*

Middle: Rear view of No 641 at Eastleigh and part of the wonderful emergency coal stack. Despite the less than perfect livery, the locomotive carrying wheel and tender axle boxes appear to have received a degree of polish. *Transport Treasury*

Bottom: Pristine condition for SR No 599 clearly soon after overhaul and repaint. It would survive until March 1946. *Transport Treasury*

By comparison, this is No 621 at Eastleigh and very possibly not long for this world – it was withdrawn in May 1935. *Transport Treasury*

A final view of No 622, location not given but Eastleigh perhaps. The former LBSCR type alongside is not identified; a 4-4-2T perhaps? Of the 90 engines of the A12 class, 77 were dismantled at Eastleigh at varying times, the remaining 13, and likely representing a fair number of the final survivors, were dealt with at Dinton. Mileages varied with a possible maximum being No 600 (12-1893 to 8-1946) which achieved a recorded 1,589,718. *Transport Treasury*

The Bluebell Railway Museum Photographic Archive.

While a small number of photographs had been collected by the Bluebell Museum from the early days, it was in 2008 that the Photographic Archive really took off. Three Bluebell members were able to purchase the John J. Smith collection. This contained many hundreds of Working Timetables, Special Traffic Notices, Carriage Working Notices plus a large negative collection.

It's probably true to say that in 2008 none of us realised the quality and importance of this collection housed in 10 shoe boxes. It was towards the end of 2008 that we started to open the shoe boxes and get samples of the negatives printed. Having now seen the quality of the images we decided to start making them available via the Bluebell Museum website. The first order was placed in February 2009.

Over the next two or three years more negatives were scanned and added to the website. This collection now totals nearly 8,000 images.

John J. Smith's collection is superb, containing numerous special and unusual workings, signal boxes and other infrastructure. The majority are of the Southern, but John travelled all over the country including industrial areas. After the Southern his next love was Ireland and there is a wonderful set of over 1,000 Irish photographs.

It was decided from Day 1 that collections would be kept together so all John's photographs, irrespective of location, are in our collection. This policy continues with later collections.

John worked for BR(S) in train planning, and it seems he created interesting workings and then went and photographed them. The M7 on

M7 No 30031 arrived at Eastbourne with empty stock on 10 July 1959 and worked the midday Hailsham train. On 12 July 1959 it worked the 9.45am Eastbourne to Tunbridge Wells West before moving to its new home at Feltham in easy stages. The photograph shows the train having just left Hellingly at 10.06am. Bluebell Museum Image Ref: 045501

T9 No 30283 somewhere between Okehampton and Padstow, it had left Okehampton at 10.15am. We do not know the actual location of this photograph. If anyone can help identify where this was taken, please let us know. Email photos@bluebell-railway-museum.co.uk *Bluebell Museum Image Ref: 040942*

the Cuckoo line image shown here is a good example of John knowing about an unusual working. He was also prepared to walk miles to take pictures well away from the usual bridge or station locations. Towards the end of steam, he must have walked between Basingstoke and Southampton to photograph the signal boxes.

Following the completion of the John J. Smith collection other collections were added. This includes Colin Hogg's collection of negatives which were already being cared for by a Bluebell member and the Southern part of the collection was next to be added. The next collection came from Alan Postlethwaite who decided to lodge his negatives in the Archive.

Joe Kent's collection followed. Joe worked in the Preston Park Pullman works and he seems to have had his camera with him continually,

even when he was later working on the roof of Brighton station. He also travelled around the Southern with his camera. Part of this collection is available with more to follow.

John Scrace was a working member of the Bluebell Museum Archive and following his death his collection is now in the Archive. John started photographing railways in the 1950s and there are 4,000 photographs of Southern stations and signal boxes. As well as steam engines John photographed EMUs and diesels. This collection is currently being added monthly to the website.

The most recent collection currently available is that of David Esau. The younger brother of Mike, David's Southern photographs are now being added to the website with his other regions to follow later in the year.

West Country No 34100 *Appledore* in charge of the Down *Golden Arrow* passes Swifts Green Signals on 25 March 1961. Swifts Green Signals was approximately halfway between Headcorn and Pluckley. It can be seen that the box board was originally made incorrectly. An 'S' has been added in the original space between Swift & Green to give the correct name. *Bluebell Museum Image Ref: 041865*

There are more collections in the pipeline including all the railway negatives from the recently acquired Jim Aston collection. J.H. Aston's photographs date from 1947 and include many electric and coaching stock images. We also have a large collection of H.C. Casserley's negatives, John Ashman's Southern negatives, and many other photographers whose names will become more familiar as we make their work available.

To access the collection, go to www.bluebell-railway-museum.co.uk and click on Archive, then Photographs. There are various ways to search including engine number and location. A 40 item 'Content Key' drop-down list gives the option of searching for *Goods Wagons, Pullmans, Sheds,* etc. This also covers southern counties. There are over 15,000 images available.

'Treasures from the Bluebell Museum' is a regular feature in Southern Times, kindly compiled by Assistant Curator Tony Hillman.

The Bluebell Railway Museum, located on Platform 2 at Sheffield Park, is well worth a visit and is a veritable treasure trove of artefacts and ephemera from the Southern Railway and its constituents. We look forward to featuring more treasures in the next issue

From records compiled by the late Alan Elliott.

	Dover									
1027	P	0-6-0T		1256	C	0-6-0		1530	H	0-4-4T
1037	C	0-6-0		1259	H	0-4-4T		1531	H	0-4-4T
1063	C	0-6-0		1261	H	0-4-4T		1532	H	0-4-4T
1070	R	0-6-0T		1263	H	0-4-4T		1555	P	0-6-0T
1101	R1	0-6-0T		1264	H	0-4-4T		1556	P	0-6-0T
1107	R1	0-6-0T		1265	H	0-4-4T		1557	P	0-6-0T
1108	O1	4-4-0		1269	H	0-4-4T		1630	U	2-6-0
1125	R	0-6-0T		1298	C	0-6-0		1631	U	2-6-0
1127	R1	0-6-0T		1307	H	0-4-4T		1632	U	2-6-0
1128	R1	0-6-0T		1323	P	0-6-0T		1633	U	2-6-0
1145	D1	4-4-0		1325	P	0-6-0T		1634	U	2-6-0
1153	R	0-6-0T		1329	H	0-4-4T		1635	U	2-6-0
1154	R1	0-6-0T		1340	R1	0-6-0T		1682	C	0-6-0
1155	R	0-6-0T		1340	R1	0-6-0T		1777	L	4-4-0
1178	P	0-6-0T		1378	O1	0-6-0		1778	L	4-4-0
1189	F	4-4-0		1390	O1	0-6-0		1779	L	4-4-0
1243	C	0-6-0		1445	R1	0-6-0T		1780	L	4-4-0
1246	D1	4-4-0		1470	D1	4-4-0		1781	L	4-4-0
1247	D1	4-4-0		1487	D1	4-4-0				

P class 0-6-0T No 1555 recorded at Rolvendon on 5 August 1947 in company with an unidentified 'Terrier'. In 1933 it was a Dover based engine and was no doubt employed on the docks lines. *Transport Treasury*

Faversham											
1017	B1	4-4-0		1379	O1	0-6-0		1502	D1	4-4-0	
1027	P	0-6-0T		1430	O1	0-6-0		1505	D1	4-4-0	
1106	O1	0-6-0		1442	B1	0-6-0T		1572	C	0-6-0	
1183	F1	4-4-0		1452	B1	0-6-0T		1584	C	0-6-0	
1186	B1	4-4-0		1461	C	0-6-0		1673	R	0-6-0T	
1217	B1	4-4-0		1486	C	0-6-0		1674	R	0-6-0T	
1221	C	0-6-0		1489	D1	4-4-0		1696	R1	0-6-0T	
1242	C	0-6-0		1492	D1	4-4-0		1697	R1	0-6-0T	
1271	C	0-6-0		1494	D1	4-4-0		1698	R1	0-6-0T	
1369	O1	0-6-0									

	Gillingham						
953	Z	0-8-0T		1510	C	0-6-0	
1003	O1	0-6-0		1574	D	4-4-0	
1007	O1	0-6-0		1585	D	4-4-0	
1043	F1	4-4-0		1654	H2	0-6-0	
1075	D	4-4-0		1657	H2	0-6-0	
1078	F1	4-4-0		1660	R	0-6-0T	
1090	C	0-6-0		1663	R	0-4-4T	Motor Train fitted
1092	D	4-4-0		1665	R	0-4-4T	Motor Train fitted
1232	F1	4-4-0		1668	R	0-4-4T	Motor Train fitted
1238	O1	0-6-0		1669	R	0-4-4T	Motor Train fitted
1274	H	0-4-4T		1670	R	0-4-4T	Motor Train fitted
1276	H	0-4-4T		1685	C	0-6-0	
1278	H	0-4-4T		1688	C	0-6-0	
1308	H	0-4-4T		1692	C	0-6-0	
1310	H	0-4-4T		1713	C	0-6-0	
1311	H	0-4-4T		1728	D	4-4-0	
1312	H	0-4-4T		1729	D	4-4-0	
1396	O1	0-6-0		1731	D	4-4-0	
1434	O1	0-6-0		1732	D	4-4-0	
1446	R1	0-6-0T		1742	D	4-4-0	
1447	R1	0-6-0T		1744	D	4-4-0	
1448	R1	0-6-0T		2495	E4	0-6-2T	
1493	D	4-4-0		2500	E4	0-6-2T	
1496	D	4-4-0		2507	E4	0-6-2T	
1501	D	4-4-0		2560	E4	0-6-2T	

1933 Faversham engine No 1186, a member of the B1 class. Undated, the engine appears in fine external condition but was withdrawn from service and scrapped in 1935. *Transport Treasury*

This time we see F1 4-4-0 No 1078 at Ashford on an unreported date. In 1933 it was shedded at Gillingham. *Transport Treasury*

	Maidstone East								
1053	F1	4-4-0		1133	F1	4-4-0		1230	F1	4-4-0
1114	F1	4-4-0		1188	F1	4-4-0		1233	F1	4-4-0
1130	F1	4-4-0		1197	F1	4-4-0				

	Maidstone West								
1014	O1	0-6-0		1337	R1	0-6-0T		1700	R1	0-6-0T
1031	F1	4-4-0		1371	O1	0-6-0		1704	R1	0-6-0T
1032	F1	4-4-0		1373	O1	0-6-0		1707	R1	0-6-0T
1069	R1	0-6-0T		1675	O1	0-6-0		2259	D1	0-4-2T
1205	F1	4-4-0		1699	R1	0-6-0T		2273	E4	0-6-2T
1231	F1	4-4-0								

	Ramsgate								
797	N15	4-6-0		1158	H	0-4-4T		1545	D1	4-4-0
798	N15	4-6-0		1161	H	0-4-4T		1554	H	0-4-4T
799	N15	4-6-0		1184	H	0-4-4T		1681	C	0-6-0
800	N15	4-6-0		1239	H	0-4-4T		1693	C	0-6-0
801	N15	4-6-0		1248	O1	0-6-0		1727	D1	4-4-0
802	N15	4-6-0		1295	H	0-4-4T		1735	D1	4-4-0
803	N15	4-6-0		1316	O1	0-6-0		1736	D1	4-4-0
804	N15	4-6-0		1322	H	0-4-4T		1739	D1	4-4-0
900	V	4-4-0		1509	D1	4-4-0		1741	D1	4-4-0
901	V	4-4-0		1518	H	0-4-4T		1743	D1	4-4-0
902	V	4-4-0		1519	H	0-4-4T		1745	D1	4-4-0
1004	C	0-6-0		1520	H	0-4-4T		1747	D1	4-4-0
1016	H	0-4-4T		1543	H	0-4-4T		1749	D1	4-4-0
1044	O1	0-6-0								

Opposite top: O1 0-6-0 No 1369, one of three examples of the type based at Faversham in 1933. *Transport Treasury*

Opposite bottom: We conclude with a pre-war view of Ramsgate shed. *Transport Treasury*

Next time: Reading, Redhill, St.Leonards and Tonbridge.

Right: Totally unrelated to engine allocations, but readers of Issue 2 will recall the question we raised on,' is it or is it not Scotland...?' (See 'From the Footplate on page 77.) 'Where it is is obviously a popular topic, so for amusement only - no prize other than the satisfaction of perhaps knowing you were the first to respond - can anyone tell us where this is please? Genuinely we have no idea. Believed Southern and of particular interest presumably a private siding training into the running line beyond the bridge. We look forward to your replies.

A Surrey-Sussex line: Horsham to Guildford Part 1

The lamented route between the two towns mentioned in the title has in the past been mainly referred to as starting from Guildford and described south to Horsham. However in this piece we have taken the description from a short series of arterioles that appeared in the Southern Region Magazine, September and October 1949 under the title 'A Surrey-Sussex Line - The Horsham-Guildford Line'. The pieces were attributed to John Gray, a gentlemen about whom we regretfully know nothing.

Twice on Sundays and eight times on lawful days a small tank engine quenches its thirst by kind permission of the Horsham stationmaster and generally prepares itself for an excursion into the realms of romance. As the London-Bognor expresses flash by with a deafening roar that draws attention to their sleek luxuriousness, one is inclined to cast aspersions on the dignity of our own little engine.

At last all is ready, the clock ticks round to the appointed second, our inconspicuous champion hisses a war cry at his aristocratic cousins of the main line, a shrill whistle pierces the air and we are off. And off we certainly are, for our champion, his pent-up energy released, canters off at a pace which would not disgrace a more pretentious giant of the railroad. Spring is in the air as well as on the railway banks and it is a pleasure to hear the whistles of joy emitted from our engine as he echoes our dumb appreciation of the yellow and blue carpeted banks. The River Arun, as yet in its infancy, flows beneath us, placidly making its way west before re-joining us near Rudgwick on its way to the sea. And so we grace the

Christ's Hospital with a Horsham to Guildford train entering the branch platform. On the opposite side of the line was the connection to the Steyning line, although as both these routes faced towards Horsham through running between Guildford and Shoreham was not possible without a reverse shunt move. Main line services still survive but both branches disappeared some years ago.

main line for another two miles through pleasant country until we reach Christ's Hospital Station. Christ's Hospital Station is the baby of the Guildford-Horsham line and indeed owes its very existence to the re-establishment of its namesake, the famous London public school in the neighbourhood.

After being domiciled in London since the time of Edward VI, there was a public outcry when it was suggested that the school should be moved into the country. Towards the close of the 19th century, however, opposition was finally quelled and the choice rested between sites in the vicinity of Wimbledon and Horsham. Needless to say the two railway companies serving the areas in question were more than a little interested in the Governors' decision, for Christ's Hospital was then a day school, which spelled a minor passenger boom for the lucky company. The Duke of Cambridge was a vigorous advocate for Wimbledon and the London and South Western Railway Company backed him up to the hilt with an offer to build a modern station in the proximity of the school. At this stage however, the London, Brighton and South Coast Railway Company, who began to see their prospective stream of passengers vanishing before their eyes, suddenly woke up to the situation and outbid their rivals with a magnificent gesture. The present spacious edifice which was opened in 1902, the year Christ's Hospital vacated their ancestral Newgate Street home for the rural seclusion of West Horsham, is the outcome of that promise. Unfortunately the London, Brighton and South Coast Railway did not long enjoy their triumph, for the school's Governors made the momentous decision to turn Christ's Hospital into a boarding school. Furthermore they refused to accept day scholars, thus foiling the Railway Company's plans to foster a new dormitory town in the district for parents working in London. Indeed, not only did the Governors turn away prospective customers from the Railway Company, but as the trustees of the surrounding countryside they stifled any development a main line railway station invariably brings in its wake. Thus we have the anomaly of a huge modern station with no

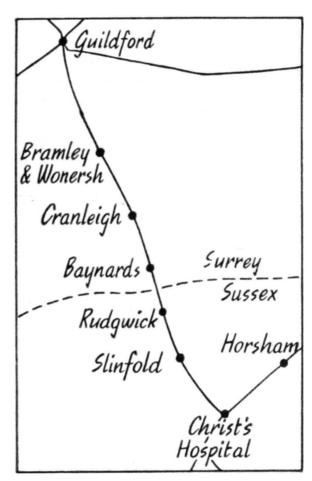

shop, hotel or public house within the vicinity, and no local industry save education.

For six days out of each year Christ's Hospital Station staggers under an avalanche of luggage and struggling humanity. At the start and end of each term it is invaded by hordes of blue-coat boys wearing the traditional knickerbockers and yellow stockings, a costume peculiar to the Christ's Hospital scholars since the school's foundation in the mid-16th century. A special train for London carries away and brings back the bulk of Christ's Hospital's population, but many still remain to crowd the local lines in which this station specialises and bring a welcome spot of pageantry to their local Sussex towns and villages.

Mr. Bonny, Christ's Hospital's amiable stationmaster, had nothing but praise for the boys' behaviour. He admitted that when he was transferred here from Crowhurst six

Far left: Former signalman Charlie Blunden who retired in February 1949 with 48 years' service on the LBSCR, SR and finally with BR(S). He had worked the signal box at Christ's Hospital for the previous 30 years. *Southern Region Magazine*

Left: Mr. and Mrs. Mussard who were based at Slinfold and lived in the station house. Ted Mussard was the sole remaining member of the traffic department staff at Slinfold; a far cry from when there had once been five employees including a stationmaster. *Southern Region Magazine*

months ago he suffered slight foreboding before his initial rush day, but added with due emphasis, "the boys behaved wonderfully".

I was interested to hear of the smooth liaison which exists between station and school. Shortly before this mass end-of-term exodus the master in charge of each house sends a list of the tickets and luggage members of his house will require to the stationmaster, thus obviating queues and ensuring that overworked booking clerks retain their sanity. Although this arrangement has proved itself of benefit to both the interested parties, it does little to relieve the volume of work which is so great as to warrant the help of two extra clerks for a week. On the great day itself, two extra porters report to Christ's Hospital to lend a hand with loading what, Mr. Bonny estimates, as approximately 600 cases and trunks. I arrived at Christ's Hospital early on that dreaded day when, holidays ended, the boys troop back to school. An astounding sight greeted my eyes, for on platform 1 was piled tier after tier of boxes, cases and trunks, all arrayed with neat precision along the wall. To gain the car park through the booking hall, I walked through a towering monument of assorted luggage awaiting collection. As befits a self-contained community, Christ's Hospital School collect their own luggage, a responsibility few will envy them. The only pre-

school railway building at Christ's Hospital is the signal box formerly known as the Stammerham Junction Box. Charlie Blunden, who only retired at the end of February, has 30 years' association with this box, during which time he has amassed considerable local knowledge and a host of staunch friends. Joining the London, Brighton and South Coast Railway Company on February 16, 1901, at Baynards, he saw service at Billingshurst, Faygate, Holmwood, Ockley, and Horsham before being transferred to Christ's Hospital in February, 1919. He showed me, with ill-concealed pride, the handsome brown initialled leather wallet presented to him, on the occasion of his retirement, by his workmates. The sincere tributes paid at this informal little gathering had evidently affected the old signalman, for on his own admission, "this wallet goes everywhere with me".

Inside were several pounds-worth of crisp temptation, but I venture to forecast that it will be a long time before Signalman Charles Edward Blunden disturbs a single note of his precious presentation wallet. Platforms 3 and 4 at Christ's Hospital form a pronounced "V", and it is from the right-angled platform 4 that the lone Guildford track celebrates its independence by swinging almost violently to the right. A single line, doubled at stations for passing purposes, and worked by the tablet system.

Mr. Bonny is also in charge of Slinfold and Rudgwick stations and has to visit his outlying satellites three times a week, which, owing to the poor train service over this line, takes up three full mornings' work. He was bound for Rudgwick on his routine tour of inspection and so we joined forces for the next two-and-a-half miles. He proved himself a very keen and vigorous administrator, jealous of the railway's interests in a district which has been systematically blooded by the road transport for a number of years now. We were very impressed by the pastoral beauty through which our unpretentious little engine was leading us. The railway banks continued to be laden with primroses and violets whilst the scattered farmhouses merged with unobtrusive character into a delicately moulded pattern of sheer enchantment. These old farmhouses, with their towering chimney stacks, are a feature of the countryside, which in olden times was a dark foreboding forest.

Slinfold Station occupies a single platform to the west of a level crossing. In the station house resides Ted Mussard and his wife, who between them keep the railway flag flying at Slinfold. There is a little of everything to do at this station. Ted is his own signalman, porter, goods porter, booking clerk, in fact the general factotum of Slinfold Station. Within the memory of Slinfold's Permanent Way Foreman Stevens, the station staff consisted of a stationmaster, two clerks, and two porter-signalmen. Now Mr. and Mrs. Mussard rule the roost in splendid isolation, and if the traffic continues its steady slump, that phrase really will be applicable.

The traffic returns for January, February and March this year are most revealing. During these three months only 470 passenger tickets were issued, and five season tickets, giving us an average of five or six ordinary passengers a day, to which may be added the faithful season ticket holders.

Several factors are instrumental in this decline, chief being the old bogey road transport which,

Slinfold looking south. Reading the original article by Mr. Gray, one cannot also be struck by the comment that taking note of local knowledge might well have assisted in developing more traffic. It may not have totally staved off the inevitable but in the 1960s the boom in population, private motoring and with it associated congestion could never have been foreseen.
Edward Wallis

Baynards bathed in late afternoon sunshine. *Graham Smith courtesy Richard Sissons.*

with an hourly bus service to Horsham, has a distinct advantage over the eight times a day railway service. The older generation of villagers recall days of frequent trains, many of which have been irretrievably lost to the modern timetable. One favourite which retained its place into the early years of the war before being withdrawn, was the 9.30 p.m. from Horsham. This enabled the local inhabitants to visit the evening pictures at Horsham or, in the summer, make a real day of it by the seaside. They brusquely dismiss the 7.12 p.m. as performing neither of these functions. It is a vexed problem, but one that may well be solved by the new British Railways' enlightened policy of attracting ramblers to the more delectable of their rural stations. Increased traffic would provide the necessary excuse for a more competitive train service and certainly the Horsham-Guildford line justifies the confidence of any rambler who essays to venture on to its territory.

Slinfold, for instance, is an ideal centre for rambling excursions. Stane Street, the ancient Roman road from Londinium (London) to Regnum (Chichester), lies about a quarter of a mile west of Slinfold Station and may be followed, with occasional lapses, across country to Ockley. We first strike the old highway whilst it is merged with the modern London - Bognor Regis road, but within a mile or so their alliance terminates and, instead of forking left or right with the motor transport, we follow our noses in a direct line by taking the Rowhook track. At Rowhook, Stane Street was joined by a subsidiary road which linked the Roman station at Farley Heath with civilisation. From Rowhook, Stane Street takes to the country, rejoining the modern highway at Halehouse Farm, which is two miles short of Ockley. A delightful, if somewhat strenuous ramble. It is of interest to note that the construction of Stane Street was begun in the 1st century, and its wonderful state of preservation is a credit to Belinus, the engineer whose name is worthily commemorated in Billingshurst and Billingsgate. Slinfold Church was a shock to me. I came prepared to see "a church of almost suburban solidity and complete want of Sussex feeling", and what I saw was an imposing church with a charming spire which is a landmark in the district. Mr. E. V. Lucas, that energetic and sincere authority of Sussex highways and byways, was the author of the foregoing quotation, and for that reason I am still a little hazy as to whether we saw the same church. At all events we saw the same village, a delightful spot whose placid exterior belies its 1,150 population. Major St. John, the Squire of Slinfold, is without doubt the greatest living authority on Slinfold. Whatever aspect of the village's social or economic history you may be interested in, Major St. John knows the answer. His father, the late Colonel St. John, sold the Slinfold section of land to the Horsham and Guildford Direct Railway Company in 1862. It was a private company incorporated in 1860, with powers to develop the country between Horsham and Guildford. Their agents were William MacCormick, M.P., Parliament Street, Westminster, and James Holmes, 109, Mount Pleasant, Liverpool. By 1864, just over 15½ miles of new track had been laid, connecting Stammerham, West Horsham with Peasmarsh, Guildford.

Both the London, Brighton and South Coast, and the London and South Western Railway companies watched the Horsham and Guildford line grow into reality with quickening interest. Tentative offers were broached by both companies, but the London, Brighton and South Coast Railway grew bold and made a firm bid to buy the Horsham and Guildford Direct Railway Company lock, stock and barrel. The deal went through and with great ceremony the line was opened on October 2, 1865. Loud and long was the jubilation in the London, Brighton and South Coast camp, for here was a legitimate excuse to poach their rival's preserves at Guildford. Meanwhile, oblivious of the complications and implications of 19th century railway politics, local villages and hamlets along the line went gay.

Slinfold's oldest inhabitant, Mrs. Anne Garman, who will be 96 on December 2, remembers seeing the first public train pass by this station. Free rides for all was the order of the day and she assures me that to local people of her generation the steam engine was as great an attraction as the jet propelled aeroplane is today. Some accounts tell of a flower garlanded train and lavishly decorated stations, but Mrs. Garman regards these as "rather fanciful". In those days Slinfold enjoyed its own stationmaster, and Mrs. Garman has vivid memories of the first, a Mr. Creecy. This gentleman, who was quite elderly when he took charge of Slinfold Station, greatly offended the God-fearing villagers by an irregular attendance at church. On being questioned as to his reasons, the old gentleman barked "I won't go to church and be late for dinner!" Mrs. Garman's husband George was one of Slinfold Station's first staff. A year or so after the inaugural opening of the line it was decided to increase the staff and so Mr. Creecy, the stationmaster, went to see if young George Garman would fill the vacant position. He found George decorating Slinfold Lodge, put the proposition to him straight away, and received another entrant into the service. But as far as Slinfold Station was concerned it was a very special entrant, for George Garman was destined to serve the London, Brighton and South Coast Railway Company at Slinfold until his death in 1913, within a few months of reaching retiring age.

Part 2 will appear in issue 4.

Opposite top: So what is the more interesting; the approaching train or the photographer…? Evidently not the train on this occasion, a 6-PUL entering Brighton in September 1964 with a fast service from Victoria routed via the Quarry line. *Graham Smith courtesy Richard Sissons*

Opposite bottom: Still on the Brighton line but in November 1962, a slow service – this time calling at rather than by-passing Redhill, in the form of 4-LAV No 2953. The train is heading south and is just passing Copyhold Junction where the line to Ardingly diverges…. . *Graham Smith courtesy Richard Sissons*

This page, top: And speaking of Ardingly in October 1963, this is the station west towards Horsted Keynes. Perhaps one day the heritage Bluebell line will make the connection back to this point. *Graham Smith courtesy Richard Sissons*

This page, bottom: Boat train for Folkestone from Victoria passing Tonbridge having run via Herne Hill and Orpington. 13 cars with an MLV at the head. Rationalisation in the form of wagon load freight and trackwork had yet to occur. The view is undated but at a guess early to mid-1960s. *Graham Smith courtesy Richard Sissons*

We are delighted to see our postbag is growing. Thank you all for your worthy contributions.

We start with a note from Julian – sorry surname not known – on the subject of the EMUs shown in the siding on page 74 of Issue 1. 'It has only just dawned on me that this photo shows the two sidings at the country end of Epsom Station. Terminating trains from Waterloo would arrive on the Down platform, and then get the shunting signal to move into the siding (on the left with the SUB train). Once the crew had changed ends, the driver could press a button which told the signalman (in the wonderful spider-like signal box which straddled the platforms) that the train was ready to move into the Up platform and head back to Waterloo via Ewell West. I think the same procedure happened with trains from Victoria into the other siding (with the EPB train).'

Julian adds, 'I expect you have already been told all this already…' We had not, so thank you.

Next from a long time and appreciated friend, Mick Field, 'Kevin, glad to see you have bounced back so quickly. Enjoyed the magazine, which looks set to be a fitting successor. I have started an index for it, as I did for SW at s548745873.websitehome.co.uk/ msrsourcev2/tpagesrs/tsoutherntimes.html

Mick adds, 'I hope we don't mind…?' Mind? Certainly not, I am honoured and I am sure like others it will be appreciated. I have used the old index many times in the past.

Mick continues, 'Odd things happen. In the *Daily Mail* a few weeks back someone asked if there were any stations between two tunnels. Well that brought back memories of my youth at Tunbridge Wells. We owned a village store and my father and I would go to Tunbridge Wells station each morning to pick up the papers from Percival Marshall the wholesalers.

So there we all were (each paper shop, etc., collect their own) standing on the Down platform. Then with much noise and steam the locomotive would burst out of the tunnel, brakes squealing. Pandemonium erupted as bundles of papers were thrown out on to the platform to be sorted, counted and piled up for each of us shops. Next of course the train would move off in to the tunnel at the end of the platform.

'Now you are going to ask what locomotives were used and where was the final destination of the train? Sad to say I was so tied up with getting our papers and getting back to the shop to do my own paper round, and of course get my breakfast before going to school, that I never did take notice. The evening paper train was less pandemonium as much fewer evening papers were sold. However Percival Marshall had, in their little office on the platform, a hand printing press. This was for late news and was printed in red ink on the back page, having been phoned down after the main issue had come off the presses….. . If only I hadn't wanted my breakfast so.'

Now from Graham Bowring about my earlier comment elsewhere on 'Jubilee' signals, especially the one at Fullerton Junction. 'To confirm, I'm fairly sure that these signals on the tall lattice bracket were installed in 1897, hence the nickname (not 1887). I don't have any documents or evidence to prove it, but what I do know is that the Hurstbourne - Fullerton line was equipped with wooden post signals when opened in 1885, and that in the late 1890s, lattice brackets such as that at Fullerton Junction were being installed around the LSW system. They were often referred to in contemporary official documents as iron signals.'

Last but by no means least, from Ralph Gilham, referring to my recent article (elsewhere) on the Sentinel Railcar and the Dyke branch.

Almost new Hastings DEMU No 1018 entering Tunbridge Wells Central station on 12 April 1958 with a Charing Cross to Hastings service. In the background is the 823yd Wells tunnel and at the opposite end of the platform was the 287yd Grove Hill tunnel. *Transport Treasury*

'Just a few additional notes I have picked up over the years about this fascinating vehicle and the people who worked on it.

'It's most regular driver on the Dyke run was Arthur (Bob) Rosea, he loved it and would be happy to swap turns to get his hands on the Railcar. (I wonder if the picture in the article is him - he looks quite at home in the cab of the leading end?) It was said that the failure in traffic on the Dyke branch was due to overloading that broke the frame.

'In 1947 Ashford works held its Centenary exhibition publishing a lavish, for the times, booklet that included aerial photographs and a full detailed fold out plan of the entire works. In one of the aerial photos the Railcar is seen in its final resting place just outside the light machine shop's north facing doors, where later in 1949 the gutted shell, still on its unique bogies, was finally dismantled.

'Regarding the fate of the Waterloo & City coaches taken to Eardley sidings in 1940.
I lived in Thornton Heath in 1941 and remember seeing a train of these top and tailed by Southern Pillbox goods brake vans on their way to Horley where they were broken up in sidings just south of the station. The other two grounded bodies remained at Eardley where I saw them in August 1948 as the fireman of E1 class No 1504 double heading with No 1735 on the empty stock of the Queen Mary boat train from Clapham Junction, a round-the-houses job.

'My memories originate from my Grandfather who lived in Junction Road, Eastbourne. He was a railway enthusiast, taking the *Railway Magazine* from issue No 1 in 1897.

Unfortunately he donated them to the salvage collection during WW2 but kept the colour plates which he gave to me as a collection.

'I can recall staying at his house in 1935 when I was about two and a half and being taken through streets that no longer exist today to Eastbourne station to meet my father who was coming by steam train. The electric service had not yet started and I saw his train arrive at the most easterly platform, later filled in to provide more additional parking spaces.

'The train was hauled by a large tank engine with two distinctive features, a pronounced rounded cab and a flat area in front of the cab where steam was issuing lazily from a squat safety valve casting. An image that I carried in my mind for years and later identified as one of the two last Baltic tanks running in their original form up to the time of the 1935 electrification and certainly also my earliest Railway memory.

'This was followed by a visit to the Isle of Wight in July 1937 and riding along Ryde Pier in the Railcar No 2, now restored and running again although of course not on the Pier.

'About the same time I walked the old Stokes Bay branch and can remember the yellow coloured curtains in the upstairs window of the crossing keeper's house near the Pier. We then watched as Fairey Swordfish bi-planes flew past dropping their dummy torpedoes that a little steam fired launch lassoed and towed back to a small crane mounted on the Admiralty owned pier. Here they hoisted it on to a platelayer's truck and trundled along the remaining railway track to the landward end where they were loaded on to an old Thornycroft lorry and taken back to be used again another day.

'Currently and for the last 15 years I have been writing for the Brighton Atlantic project supporters journal about my involvement with Southern locomotives as engine cleaner and fireman from Southern Railway days and into the BR era at Stewarts Lane Depot.'

Now to 'that' photograph - page 2 ST2.

We start with Martin Bardbeer. 'Hello, Just got the latest issue of Southern Times (ST2) and only opened as far as page 2 so far! The location of the photo with 32096 is Barnstaple Junction, at the southern (up) end of platform 1. The loco is standing at the coaling siding. The track to the right is a siding leading to the goods shed (behind the photographer).

Although there is a platform edge, this was never given a platform number and no passenger trains left from it, although there was a Mortehoe to Waterloo summer Saturday train that collected a restaurant car from the platform. I must have spent many hours at or near this spot in the early 1960s

The head code is from Duty 579, which had the loco on station pilot and yard duty at Barnstaple Junction, with a trip to Fremington to shunt wagons on the quay for the afternoon. I see that 32096 went from Barnstaple Junction to Plymouth Friary in June 1955 before being withdrawn from Friary in November 1956. So your picture has to be before 1955 (and that was about when I first got taken to Barnstaple Junction to watch the trains!)

I really enjoyed issue 1 and I am sure that issue 2 will not disappoint.'

Along similar lines from Martin James. 'Hello Southern Times … I'm enjoying Issue 2 and I love "mystery photos" …

'There is no mystery about the photo of 32096 on Page 2 … it is at its home shed of Barnstaple Junction - 72E. It's sitting on the engine shed road next to the coal stage. There are lots of clues - one being the signal on the platform and another being the signal in the middle distance (to the right of the loco) which is the home signal for the line from Barnstaple Victoria Road. No. 32096 was based at Barnstaple Junction between May 1949 and June 1955. After 1955 it moved to Plymouth Friary shed until withdrawn in October 1956. Most of the E1/R locos were replaced by LMS Type 2 2-6-2 tank locos - examples at Barnstaple Shed being 41295 / 7 / 8.'

Another correspondent was Roger Merry-Price. 'Barnstaple Junction Duty No. 579 (on the loco's disc) was for an E1/R and depending on the date would cover duties to Torrington and on to Halwill Junction or shunting at Fremington.

'Barnstaple Junction with the left signal controlling the spur around to Barnstaple Victoria Road.'

Thanks also to similar from Tony Hillman.